ALSO BY SAM PINK

No One Can Do Anything Worse To You Than You Can

The No Hellos Diet

Hurt Others

Person

The Self-Esteem Holocaust Comes Home

I Am Going to Clone Myself Then Kill the Clone and Eat It

Some of these poems, in present form or otherwise, have appeared in your head when you disgust yourself most.

2007 - 2009

Lazy Fascist Press

Lazy Fascist Press
An Imprint of Eraserhead Press
205 NE Bryant Street
Portland, Oregon 97211

www.lazyfascistpress.com

ISBN: 978-1-62105-044-5

Copyright © 2010, 2012 by Sam Pink

Cover art copyright © 2010, 2012 by Sam Pink

Cover design by Matthew Revert
www.matthewrevert.com

All rights reserved. No part of this book may be reproduced or transmitted in any form or by any means, electronic or mechanical, including photocopying, recording, or by any information storage and retrieval system, without the written consent of the publisher, except where permitted by law.

Printed in the USA.

TABLE OF CONTENTS

001   INTRODUCTION BY JEREME DEAN

003   I HEART UNENDING PARANOIA

004   PUBERTY

006   DURING SEXUAL INTERCOURSE I ENVISION MY OWN BRUTAL DEATH

007   CONSTANT STARING

008   I CAN IMITATE A FLOOR

009   I WOULD DRINK A MOUTHFUL OF WATER THAT IS A MOUTHFUL OF WATER A THOUSAND OTHER PEOPLE HAVE PASSED FROM MOUTH TO MOUTH

011   NO-JOY HEADLESS ADOLESCENT

012   MY ROOM IS NOT AN EYELESS SHAPE THAT IS TRYING TO EAT ME

013   I WASTE TIME BY THINKING ABOUT THE FUTURE IN DETAIL

014   BE LAUGHY

015   ABUSIVE ROMANCE-PARTNER

017   CHICAGO ASSHOLE ALL-STAR

018   THE NAP

019   UNDYING ACCIDENT-BIRTH PULLED FROM BETWEEN BROKEN LEGS

020	PERSON IN A WHEELCHAIR ON A TRAMPOLINE
021	SOME PEOPLE HAVE PERSONALITIES THAT ARE COMB-OVERS
022	PISS-BUSH
024	I CAN'T THINK OF A TITLE FOR THIS BECAUSE MY ATTENTION SPAN IS DISAPPEARING (NOT JOKING, I'M CONCERNED)
025	BE JEALOUS
026	HEIL ME!
027	FRUIT SNACKS
029	MY LITTER-SKULL
030	SOMETHING TELLS ME I'M GOING TO DIE IN AN ALLEY
032	CHESTHAIR TOUPEE
033	THE EARTH SNIFFED PAINT WHILE IT WAS PREGNANT WITH ME
034	NOT WEARING UNDERWEAR MAKES ME HORNY
036	I SAW A DEAD BODY ON THE CORNER OF ASHLAND AND ROOSEVELT AND I WALKED BY IT AND THERE ARE SIXTEEN VERSIONS OF WHAT HAPPENED
039	A CAREER OF LOOKING TIRED
040	WAITING FOR SOMEONE TO LOOK AT ME AND SAY, "WHAT'S WRONG" (THEN I BLACK OUT, REMEMBERING NOTHING)
042	"SUCKS ASS" WOULD BE A FUNNY WAY TO DESCRIBE SOMEONE'S HAIRCUT IF ASKED FOR AN OPINION

043	I LIKE WHEN SOMEONE ELSE SCRATCHES MY CHEST
045	SCREAMING FACE
046	SOME SHIT ABOUT WHAT I'D DO WITH TIME TRAVEL
047	DON'T CONFUSE THE MARCH OF THE THING YOU HATE FOR HOW IT BLINKS ITS EYES AT YOU
048	UNTITLED
049	BECAUSE YOU KNOW YOU'RE AVOIDING GOING SOMEWHERE BUT YOU DON'T EVEN KNOW WHERE YET
051	THE QUICK VERSION OF HOW TO BE SUCCESSFUL
052	THE INTRUDERS ARE REAL AND THEY ARE GOING TO KILL ME IF I STOP PROTECTING MYSELF
054	LOVE STORY
055	DEATH
056	IN THE LAST TWO YEARS I HAVE TALKED TO ANIMALS OR MYSELF MORE THAN I HAVE TALKED TO OTHER HUMANS
058	WHAT IT IS, MOTHERFUCKERS
059	I HAVE A PROBLEM WITH RANDOM LAUGHING
060	YOUR EMBRYO
062	BIPOLAR IDIOT
063	DICKHOLE
065	WANTING OTHER PEOPLE TO THINK LIKE YOU IS DUMB
066	I'M NOT GOING TO CHANGE MY CLOTHES TODAY

068	I SUCK
069	HEY, MOLE ON THE LOWER BACK/UPPER ASSCHEEK OF THE GIRL STANDING IN FRONT OF ME AT THE POST OFFICE
071	NO TOLERANCE
072	FOUR APOLOGIES
073	HEY LEG-PINCHER, HOP ON MY BACK, I'M HORNY-NICE RIGHT NOW
074	FOR SOME THINGS, THERE IS NO ERASER
076	FEELING LIKE SHIT WAS AROUND BEFORE HUMAN BEINGS
077	DON'T BE A DICK, LOVE ME
078	IT IS WEIRD TO BE AT A HOUSEPARTY WHERE EVERYONE IS ALIVE EXCEPT YOU
079	FUCK YOU, DUMMY
080	I BELIEVE IT'S OK TO PERMANENTLY DISFIGURE YOURSELF
082	EVERYTHING IS A CALENDAR
083	AT A RESTAURANT I SAW A GUY WITH A LONG-ASS BEARD (NO, NOT LONG ASS-BEARD)
085	IS VERY DIFFICULT TO UNDERSTAND WHAT OTHER PEOPLE THINK (IS VERY DIFFICULT)
087	EARLIER I THOUGHT, "CUT A BIG WOUND INTO YOUR CHEST, IT'LL BE OK"
089	I WANT TO SCREAM IN SOMEONE'S FACE AND INTIMIDATE HIM/HER

090 NEANDERTHAL CLITORIS

091 I LIKE WHEN A GIRL HAS PAINTED NAILS/ TOE-NAILS

093 I DAYDREAM ABOUT MY HANDS BECOMING LIQUID

094 SILENT DINNERS FUCKING RULE

096 A LOT OF PEOPLE LIVE IN CHICAGO (I'D SAY, A SHITLOAD)

097 I HAVE BAD URGES

098 TWO PEOPLE KICKING MY HEAD AT THE SAME TIME, ONE IN FRONT AND ONE BEHIND

099 I HAVE A BIG BUTT

100 WHEN I GO FOR WALKS I PURPOSELY BRUSH UP AGAINST BUSHES AND STREET SIGNS BECAUSE, I DON'T KNOW, IT JUST FEELS SO RIGHT

102 DON'T BE A STEREOTYPE (OR DO, I DON'T CARE)

104 REALLY BIG CARROT

105 PASSIVE DEATH ALL DAY LONG

107 UNTITLED

108 THE NAP (PART 2)

109 A CERTAIN AMOUNT OF SEX ACTUALLY FEELS BAD

111 YOU WILL NOT CELEBRATE

112 WINNERS

114	GETTING SHOT IN THE EYE WITH AN ARROW PROBABLY WON'T EVER HAPPEN TO ME (FINGERS CROSSED)
115	UNTITLED II
116	THE LAST TIME I SAID SOMETHING RACIST, IT WAS UNINTENTIONAL, I WAS IN SECOND GRADE AND I MADE MY (FIRST) MEXICAN GIRLFRIEND CRY, AND IT SUCKED
117	I SAW FLIES ALL OVER MY ROOM LAST NIGHT AND I WASN'T ON DRUGS
119	SOME PEOPLE DESERVE TO BE TREATED POORLY
120	CRUSHING IRRITATION (OUTSIDE I FEEL UGLY)
122	THE GUM ON THE FLOOR IS ME (IS ME ON THE FLOOR)
123	THE APOCALYPSE HAPPENS EVERY TIME SOMEONE DIES
125	WE ARE GOOD AT BECOMING OLDER
127	I HOPE I GIVE A CONVINCING THANK YOU TO SOMEONE BEFORE I DIE
129	BOO!
130	WHERE DOES GLITTER COME FROM, IS THERE LIKE, A MINE?
131	COPS FREAK ME OUT BECAUSE I DON'T LIKE WHEN PEOPLE TRY TO CONTROL ME
132	ELDERLY COUPLE

133	CAT SKULL
134	I WORSHIP SATAN
135	SELF-ESTEEM
136	HOLOGRAPHIC PERSONALITY DISGRACE
138	RELATIONSHIP
139	ONE THING CAN EXPLAIN EVERYTHING ELSE
140	I ALWAYS THINK, "IF I JUST GET A GOOD AMOUNT OF SLEEP I'LL BE FINE"
141	I AVOID WASHING DISHES BECAUSE I USUALLY REMEMBER SOMETHING AWFUL IN THE SILENCE
142	LITTLE KIDS AND ANIMALS LIKE ME
143	PLEASE ADOPT ME
144	I LIKE TO HURT OTHER PEOPLES' FEELINGS SOMETIMES (I MEAN SOMETIMES IT ACTUALLY FEELS LIKE THE ONLY SKILL I POSSESS ABOVE ALL OTHERS)
146	SELF-INFLICTED CONTRACEPTIVE IDEA
148	COMMIT CRIMES/KILL YOUR PARENTS/LIGHT SOMETHING ON FIRE/STEAL SOMETHING
150	IDEALLY AT SOME POINT IN MY LIFE I'D LIKE TO EMERGE FROM AN ALLEY AND STAND IN FRONT OF PEOPLE ON THE STREET AND SAY, "REAL PAIN" WITHOUT LOOKING AT ANY OF THEM, THEN RETREAT BACK INTO THE ALLEY

152	FALLING ASLEEP ON THE COUCH = FAILURE
154	PEOPLE WHO DO COCAINE ARE USUALLY FUCKHEAD DICK CULTURE
155	THERE IS NO WAY TO WASTE TIME
156	OXYGEN IS PRETTY GOOD
158	I DARE YOU NOT TO DIE WHEN I LICK THE BOTTOM OF YOUR FOOT WHILE WE ARE FUCKING
159	WHEN I MAKE A PEANUT BUTTER SANDWICH AND LOOK AT MY REFLECTION ON THE MICROWAVE I LAUGH AND GO "YOU SILLY MAN" THEN I EAT THE SANDWICH ALONE IN THE KITCHEN, LEANING MY BACK AGAINST THE COUNTER
161	IN SIXTH GRADE I WATCHED THE JANITOR BEAT MY CLASSMATE AND I LAUGHED (OH HOW I LAUGHED)
163	COMPLEX NEUROTIC VISIONARY TORTURE
164	"ASSWIPE" IS A GOOD WAY TO DESCRIBE SOME PEOPLE, OR MAYBE I AM WRONG
165	I DON'T WEAR TURTLE-NECK SHIRTS BECAUSE OF THE POWERLESS TERROR I EXPERIENCE WHEN MY HEAD GETS STUCK
167	PAINLESS, WELL-WISHER EXTINCTION
168	I'M CONFUSED WHEN PEOPLE ASK, "WHAT ARE YOU GOING TO DO TODAY."
169	SLOWLY NEGLECTING A RELATIONSHIP

170	THERE IS NOTHING TO DO
171	HAVING A CELL PHONE MAKES ME FEEL CORNERED BUT I COULD SAY THE SAME THING ABOUT HAVING EYES TOO, I THINK
172	I WONDER IF 'CLIVE JACKSON' IS THE NAME OF A REAL PERSON (IT HAS TO BE)
174	LISTENING TO MY NEIGHBORS SCREAM WHILE I DO A PUZZLE
175	I AM POSSESSED (NOT JOKING)
176	I AM NOT UPSET
177	I GET UNCOMFORTABLE AROUND PEOPLE WHO GET ANGRY AT VIDEO GAMES
178	I STILL HAVE ALL MY TEETH, HOMEY
179	EXPRESSIONLESS DISGUST IS MY NATIONALITY
180	THE BURGLAR
181	I AM HERE
182	SLEEPOVERS AT SOMEONE ELSE'S HOUSE ALWAYS SCARED ME WHEN I WAS YOUNGER BECAUSE I THOUGHT THE OTHER FAMILY WOULD SURROUND ME AND KILL ME
184	NOBODY CAN CONTROL ME
185	PIECE OF WRITING THAT IS TONALLY DIFFERENT AND ENDS THE BOOK

INTRODUCTION BY JEREME DEAN

In 2009, the Associated Writing Programs annual conference was held in Chicago. A plane ticket was purchased the day before the flight, and for a drug fueled reason I can't remember, socks were not worn or packed. It was winter.

The purpose of the visit wasn't the writing conference. The purpose of the visit was to meet two people: a 17-year old virgin I considered my soulmate; and a poet named Sam Pink. AWP itself was adjunct.

Let me be clear, I loathe the energy of writers. A banal, egotistical, shit-hearted bunch. Such company can be suffered only in small measurements, and often I found myself fleeing the conference for the sanctuary of clean air.

During one of many escapes, soulmate in tow, a man asked for spare change. Anxiety was high, and the stare towards my feet wasn't raised when I replied I had already given my dollars to another pan handler, which was a truthful answer. I felt his presence behind me, following, unaccepting. My knee-jerk reaction was to scream the man away, but I caught myself after turning to face a huge grin and a mohawk. The recognition was instant.

Sam agreed anywhere but the conference was a necessity. We made a long walk, or at least it seemed so without socks, to the Shedd Aquarium. Free admission Tuesday. The three of us entered.

The ground was hard with snow outside, the great lake desolate, the people hiding. Inside, we walked quietly from exhibit to exhibit, bearing witness to small creatures in aquatic prisons, never crossing paths with other visitors.

The silence was our bond. For once in 31 years I briefly felt not alone. I panicked a little. Sam motioned a hug when we made our goodbye, but I evaded like a terrified bitch.

Soon *Frowns Need Friends Too* was released. The book read entirely during bus commute, in two days, in Los Angeles. The not alone feeling returned, anchored, expanding like a lung cancer.

In 2012, the city of Chicago was again scheduled for AWP. I wanted to see my friend, but couldn't stomach that kabuki dick dance of a show. My soulmate and I flew to the Windy City in the autumn of 2011.

I arrived dope sick, with plenty of socks and a few tabs of LSD. There was no itinerary. Just a week to burn.

The last day Sam met with us. We smoked marijuana, walked the Loop, ate Al's Beef, and swallowed acid. It felt good to be in the company of a genuine friend.

A goodbye blunt at 3:00am was shared, followed by a hug then we left for separate ways. The thought that I may never see my friend again blossomed. I turned back to witness a juggernaut with tiny hands progressing towards an unknown destination. I emphatically yelled, "Bye, Sam!"

He didn't look back.

Maybe you're wondering what the purpose of this introduction is. It's about the poet, not the poetry. *Frowns Need Friends Too* is a thirty-four layer bean dip with a surface layer as deep as the volume of the other thirty-three layers combined. I refuse to spoil its beauty with explanation or interpretation.

The only comment I'll provide: this book is the honest laughter of a drowning prophet. Enjoy its song.

       Jereme Dean
       Hollywood, CA
       07/2012

I HEART UNENDING PARANOIA

One day I want to wake up to someone telling me s/he hates me. I want that person to follow me around all day, telling me how much s/he hates me. That person can tell me as many times as seems necessary and in any way s/he wants. At night I will cook that person dinner so s/he doesn't get too weak to keep telling me about hating me. And I will try to make sure that person gets enough blankets when we're going to sleep, so s/he doesn't get too cold to tell me how much I am hated. And I will try not to pull the blankets off in the night (even if it's totally accidental (and if I accidentally do pull off the blankets, I hope that person is not an asshole about it (or at least I hope that person is not too upset to continue telling me how much I am hated))). I need to hear it for at least a week straight to return to normal.

PUBERTY

I believe you can destroy a city with a somersault, provided the city is small enough and provided you don't have a bad back.

I believe you can trample your friends if you don't like them and I believe you can trample them or anything else in a way that makes it seem like that's not what you're doing.

I believe that no one is guilty of anything.

I believe all material objects are made of small green circles that resemble blood cells and I believe that those small green circles all look the same. And I believe you are one of the small green circles.

I wouldn't argue with someone who said I was smaller than outerspace, no.

Because I'm destined to never talk to a certain amount of the population.

That is true about you.

That is true about the rest of the population.

You can cut out a small cube of air and use it as a pillow and you can see things while you are sleeping that will make you lots of scared.

But who doesn't like a dumb scared motherfucker.

DURING SEXUAL INTERCOURSE I ENVISION MY OWN BRUTAL DEATH

The other day I went for a walk and while I was at an intersection I saw a man wearing colorful shorts.

I said, "I like your shorts."

He looked down and then back at me and paused.

He said, "Yeah, these are like, my favorite shorts. That's why I wear them so much."

I said, "Yeah, I can see why. If those were my shorts I would wear them a lot too."

He nodded and then turned and looked at the stoplight.

It was the most successful conversation I have ever had.

I thought, "Just quit now."

CONSTANT STARING

Sometimes I can't sleep because I'm thinking about all the people I have disappointed.

Sometimes I can't remember who those people are but I'm sure they are there.

Sometimes I can't sleep because I'm thinking about new and better ways to disappoint people.

Sometimes I worry there is no one left to disappoint.

I CAN IMITATE A FLOOR

When I get what I want, no one else will.

And wherever I stand, the world gets my weight.

I am meditating on the idea of my own throat cut down to the spine.

Today I walked by an old lady on the street and she said, "Kill yourself."

Shhh, no one is breathing anymore, no one is awake.

When others get what they want, what you want is changed.

I WOULD DRINK A MOUTHFUL OF WATER THAT IS A MOUTHFUL OF WATER A THOUSAND OTHER PEOPLE HAVE PASSED FROM MOUTH TO MOUTH

There is an I.V. of the times I have thought, "I don't know what I'm talking about" and it is swelling my veins.

I want to fall in front of you and make you laugh.

Everything is exactly the same.

Everyone is describing the same thing.

The only difference is what scrapes what.

A big rock becomes a small rock becomes a big rock becomes something you throw into the air becomes something you hope lands on you and kills you.

When I say mean things I am apologizing quietly in my head. And isn't it great how quiet some things are.

I like to be constantly half-damaged. I like to scrape myself and then apologize.

I am sorry I have made more people than have made me cry.

No, I'm not sorry.

How many times have you held the answer in and felt like a shitty little petty motherfucker champion.

A picture of the back of my head proves that other places exist and that I can be wrong.

And I am teenaged every few minutes.

The only son of a puddle's crater.

Look how huge I am.

Arms strong from waving goodbye to assholes.

NO-JOY HEADLESS ADOLESCENT

It is impossible to dislike someone you see sleeping.

MY ROOM IS NOT AN EYELESS SHAPE THAT IS TRYING TO EAT ME

My room is not an eyeless shape that is trying to eat me.
My room is not an eyeless shape that is trying to eat me.

I WASTE TIME BY THINKING ABOUT THE FUTURE IN DETAIL

The next time I put my weight on you will be the next time I scratch my facial hair into your neck and chest will be the next time red lines form from the scratching—composing a pretty picture—will be the next time I remember that I am going to be alive for a long long time will be the next time I remember that the meantime is meant for changing everything into something that retains the marks of my intervention will be the next time I put my weight on you.

BE LAUGHY

The underwear I want is the kind made from barely-slept eyelids.

The kindness I have is the kind pulled from deep inside the couch, where you reach and sometimes your hand gets poked.

The new facial features I made are the kind fashioned from muscles unwrapped from a sleeping ribcage.

The hand I want is the one I have and the things that go inside are what's missing.

The thing I want is what misses me.

One of us is an earthworm in a chewed-on papercup full of sand.

And the other is the person watching.

ABUSIVE ROMANCE-PARTNER

There is no night and day there are only small naps.

There is no way to understand anything there are only nods

There is no holding hands there is only making sure the other doesn't run.

There is no idea there is only saying something one of us already said but forgot about.

There are no naps there are only blinks.

There are no blinks there are only small rips in sight.

There is no fun there is only me not saying anything.

There is no floor there is only feeling like you can't go more below.

There is no washer and dryer in my apartment building and that sucks fucking balls.

There are no fingers there are only smaller pieces of your arm.

There are no arms there is only your body trying to expand

without your permission.

There are no endings there is only not wanting to continue.

CHICAGO ASSHOLE ALL-STAR

Is good feeling to just stare back at someone who has failed to make you laugh. Is good feeling.

Is ridiculous that I have to wear clothes everywhere.
Is ridiculous.

I have been alive for thousands of days.

Right now I am sweaty and I feel like I have given up.

And the only way to sleep is to not be anything else.

More of my time is spent thinking about how I could die at any moment rather than setting goals and achieving those goals.

And my goal is to be found in someone's pool.

Being dead will be the easiest thing I do.

I am not accomplishing anything—my feet are shovels and all my sperm are tailless.

Is good feeling.

THE NAP

At the grocery store today I saw a very huge woman on a motorized vehicle.

There were kids running circles around her.

When I got outside with my groceries there was snow falling and I knew the snow was disappearing when it hit the ground.

I also knew that I was at the part of the nap where I realize the nap is long. Very long.

I was at the part of the nap where I realize the nap is long and that it will end itself without my permission.

UNDYING ACCIDENT-BIRTH PULLED FROM BETWEEN BROKEN LEGS

My fingernails would make great shingles for a very small person's house.

And my chest hair would make great carpeting.

My teeth could make shovels to overturn small pieces of earth and I hope a tree grows over my grave and the roots strangle my skeleton.

I have a videotape of my conception—it is proof no god exists.

Just kidding.

I am a human with its eyes closed. And I regret everything I do.

My face is proof.

Gross.

So gross.

PERSON IN A WHEELCHAIR ON A TRAMPOLINE

I don't care if it takes me the rest of my life I am going to spit on my feet until I float away from the planet into space where there's no one to talk to and nothing to do.

You can be a miniature god if you shoot my boiling head and kill it.

Shoot my boiling head—I feel too stupid to move.

My plaque deposits become horns when I shove them deep into my forehead. Still look the same.

And I can kill anything that is smaller than my mouth or hands.

And I can become small enough to represent myself as a secret.

Yuh huh.

Everyone is describing the same thing.

SOME PEOPLE HAVE PERSONALITIES THAT ARE COMB-OVERS

1. While I was waiting for the bus I put my hand into my pocket to get some change but my fingers went through a hole in my pocket and I accidentally touched my own leg. It felt horrible. I hope that never happens again.

2. While I was waiting for the bus I put my hand into my pocket to get some change but my fingers went through a hole in my pocket and I touched air. My leg was gone. I looked at my hand. My hand was gone. My legs and feet were gone. I was a rock. Some wind blew me into the street and I made the street heavier and I forgot about the bus.

3. While I was waiting for the bus I put my hand into my pocket to get some change. I took my hand out and it was filled with ants. "That's where I put those," I said. The bus pulled up and I stared at it, ants falling out of my hand.

4. While I was waiting for the bus I put my hand into my pocket to get some change. A person walked up to the bus stop and said, "There will be room on the bus for us both because we are nothing." I nodded.

5. While I was waiting for the bus I put my hand into my pocket to get some change and I forgot where I was and what I was doing and I looked at a cloud for help but it said nothing.

PISS-BUSH

I can make a gift for you that is a snowball in a brown paperbag and I can make a gift for you that is confetti cut from lamplight and I make gifts like that, that's all I do.

I woke up facedown in my pillow and I thought the world was gone and I became a millionaire but I was wrong and now I regret throwing out all of my underwear and socks.

Being alive for a whole year seems like it deserves a commemorative plaque I think.

Sometimes if I think about breathing it becomes hard to breathe and I almost pass out.

Definitely best not to think about anything.

Definitely good to watch someone cry.

If I knew what I was doing I would stop doing it.

After I figure out how to eliminate people, I figure out how to miss them.

And a small town can become a big field if you destroy it thoroughly.

And my face hurts from frowning.

I apologize.

People act according to how many people they want to visit their grave or just think about visiting their grave.

A car crash breaks your arm but sitting still breaks your spine and some things explode without moving.

Underneath each of my fingernails are friends—on their backs with their arms and legs pointing upward—waiting to be turned over to crawl off.

Win friendships with a bad mind. Do that.

I guide a river into your sleeping ear and it comes out the other end a different color.

You get one long chance to be a failure and the fewer times you fail the bigger that chance gets.

Have a nice night and be pleased by rupturing your own blood cells.

I can't believe I am this close to the ground.

I CAN'T THINK OF A TITLE FOR THIS BECAUSE MY ATTENTION SPAN IS DISAPPEARING (NOT JOKING, I'M CONCERNED)

I have sex dreams where I hold someone and I don't have sex with them.

I have a feeling that other people are ruining my mind.

And when I visit someone it's fun to just leave when that person goes to the bathroom or goes to get something.

We're lucky no one can stand themselves individually otherwise we wouldn't be needed.

I got up a second ago and accidentally hit my finger on the doorframe and now my finger feels broken.

There is no way to be comfortable anymore.

No more fun from now on.

BE JEALOUS

I promise I will be more professional with hurting your feelings horribly and I promise when I point my finger it will have my whole boneframe behind it. I promise I am going to keep you, and give you enough water and food and care. I don't know what I am doing. But I promise I will make my head professional. I promise to be mean. There are endless ways to ruin a house but making it feel bad about itself is the quickest and most professional. Everything I think or have thought is true. Weak things collapse. Tell your friends how much you dislike them. I promise I don't know what I'm doing but I'm a professional. I promise there are more examples of how to mistreat people than anything else. I promise to professionally make you an example.

HEIL ME!

Sorry I clipped your fingernails too short but it's hard to do with scissors—please don't be mean.

You can put your fingers in my mouth I have a feeling that will make them better.

When I lick the pulp beneath your nails you will feel better and maybe I will too.

And maybe your pulp will teach my tongue new things about being soft.

Sorry about cutting your fingernails too short but I still like you a whole lot.

Sorry, but some hugs are terrible. They leave me feeling like I got soaked on my way somewhere and I like, only halfway dried off before the day was over.

What I'm trying to say is, I need to build a real forcefield around me to replace the fake one.

FRUIT SNACKS

Don't touch me—my skin is boiled by heartbroke-flies dropping tears.

I will never see all myself at once.

I will never see most of my organs.

I will never surgically remove anyone's cancer.

I will never be a greatgrandmother.

I will never teach anyone how to do complex math.

I will never give birth.

I will never jumprope off a mountain.

I will never perform a magic trick that makes someone admire me.

I try to make people laugh so for a period of a few seconds I have done nothing wrong and I owe nothing.

And the blackest color is behind your eyes.

I will never make a map of anything.

I will never stop making lifesize maps of the holding cell you make for me in your bad hopes.

I was eating some cereal and one of the marshmallows stuck to my lip and then it fell off and went beneath the couch and I am not going to look for it I think I am going to leave it there alongside the muscles I use to hold up my eyelids yeah man.

Fail in public like a petty motherfucker champion.

Fail and let it make you hard.

Yes I get hard when I put my hand on your knee.

Yes you get mad when I put my hand on your knee.

Yes I get hard when you are mad.

Yes nothing gets me hard anymore.

MY LITTER-SKULL

If you don't kill your bad thoughts, your bad thoughts will kill you.

It's the same with your pets and the same with all your relatives I guess.

SOMETHING TELLS ME I'M GOING TO DIE IN AN ALLEY

When your hand is a field it will make many things.

When your hand is a field it will be covered in dirt.

When you stand face to face with the things you've made but do not like, it will define you in some way.

And when your hand is a field your tongue is a cloud.

When there's nothing left to say I will go to sleep and you will never hear from me again.

The moment I have gained some importance in your life I will be gone—that's natural.

Yesterday I saw a squirrel run out into the street and a car ran it over.

The squirrel kind of tried to run away but just fell down.

Then the squirrel twitched once, like it was doing a sit-up.

Then it was still.

I'm glad I saw that because otherwise I would've had nothing to think about while I was sitting on the train this morning, waiting to twitch once, then be still.

CHESTHAIR TOUPEE

When someone says something to me and I'm not listening and it looks like they want a response, I act startled and point behind them and say, "Oh shit—get down."

Then I run away.

THE EARTH SNIFFED PAINT WHILE IT WAS PREGNANT WITH ME

I have to find a bed where no one will find me.

No one can know where my real bed is.

I saw a pile of leaves today and thought, "No one will find me here. Here is good for a bed."

I thought the same thing about this girl's hood while I was in line at a store but then I remembered she would probably fall over if I slept in her hood and I said, "Oh yeah" out loud and she turned and looked at me.

Everything you care about is easily lost or has to die off and you won't know how it happens until it happens.

You don't have to forget everyone you meet but you can if you want .

If you want, no one can find you.

NOT WEARING UNDERWEAR MAKES ME HORNY

The main difference between me and a caterpillar is that I will remain a disgusting bug.

The main difference between me and a pedophile is that I don't have a moustache.

Last night I sat on the curb out front of my apartment and I looked back at my apartment and realized it wasn't my home and I looked at the moon and pointed at it, making a gun motion with my finger and thumb and I smiled with one eye closed, repeating the words, "Hello, I am a bad enemy to have and an even worse friend."

My back hurts today. Put an ice cube in your mouth for a little bit then lick my back.

I cover myself in mirrors and I make no friends.

When I make friends I cover them in mirrors.

Every time I open my mouth I melt the things in front of me and every time I draw x's over my eyes I fool other people into not introducing themselves.

When you hear yourself saying something, make sure you

hear yourself as a complete enemy.

When you wake up today, treat the first thing you see like a complete enemy.

Nothing can absolve the day.

When you touch the ceiling of your scared life look at your fingers and remember the color.

Absolve the day and feel huge.

I SAW A DEAD BODY ON THE CORNER OF ASHLAND AND ROOSEVELT AND I WALKED BY IT AND THERE ARE SIXTEEN VERSIONS OF WHAT HAPPENED

1. I was walking on the sidewalk and saw a body lying in the street with a blanket over it. There were police everywhere. I think maybe the police could've situated a bunch of tissues or pillows underneath the blanket just to fool me but I don't think they would do that.

2. I walked down the street and saw a dead body lying in the street with a blanket over it. I thought about getting underneath the blanket too but I knew I wouldn't be able to stop laughing when the police loaded me into the ambulance.

3. I saw the dead body. There were a lot of people but no one was talking to each other. I crossed the street and there was a man at the other side. I looked at him and said, "It's really cold out." He said, "Yeah." And I walked past him.

4. I walked past the dead body and after I was out of sight the dead body disintegrated and floated upward in small screams that no one could hear.

5. I walked up to the dead body and the police. I looked at

one of the policemen and said, "If you want, I can lift it up and put it way high up in a tree so it's out of everybody's way." The policeman said, "For some reason the first thing I thought after you just talked to me was, 'Fuck you.'" I thanked him and told him to come get me if he needed someone to throw the dead body way up high in a tree.

6. The dead body wasn't really there I just mistook a really big puddle for a dead body.

7. I walked up to the dead body and tried to tickle its feet. It didn't move when I tickled its feet. A cop said, "I tried too—nothing."

8. I folded the dead body up when no one was looking. I put the folded dead body in my pocket. I walked away. I was so excited to see it I left it in my pocket and touched it once in a while to make sure it was still there. It was always still there. Now I don't even check.

9. I saw the dead body and walked across the street. I passed a girl on a cellphone. I think she was trying not to make eye contact with me. I understood that and appreciated that. I looked at my feet and forgot what I was supposed to be doing for the next couple of decades.

10. I walked up to the dead body and I said, "Hello, how are you." The dead body said nothing and we became best friends.

11. When I saw the dead body I turned to the policeman and said, "What do you call this again." The policeman said, "That is called a human." I said, "Oh yeah, thanks." And I walked away and I knew what a human looked like. I saw them everywhere.

12. I walked up to the dead body and the policeman and I played a few games of tic-tac-toe on the dead body and the policeman kept winning because he kept taking the middle spot like a cheating motherfucker.

13. I walked up to the dead body and lay down next to it and I put my arm around it and said, "What time do you have work tomorrow, honey."

14. I stopped next to the dead body. A policeman looked at me. I smiled and said, "You will do just as good a job as this person is doing, don't worry." The policeman said, "I am the same thing standing up."

15. I walked up to the body. I looked at it. I bent down and scooped some water from a puddle. I put the water up to the dead body's mouth. Nothing happened. I thought, "I am going to go watch tv," and then I walked away and my hand was cold and wet.

16. I came up to the dead body and I looked at it. I could tell where the nose was under the blanket and where the mouth was too. When I tried to imagine more, it became impossible. I wanted to lift the blanket but I knew how cold the body would be without the blanket. I didn't feel anything else. I didn't care. I still don't care. Everyone is fine where they're at.

A CAREER OF LOOKING TIRED

When I wake up, I stay completely still and say, "Yayyyy" for as long as I can with one breath.

Yesterday I acted like the lightbulb in my room was the sun and outside my door there were too many evil people waiting for me, so I didn't leave.

I did good acting.

I did good acting for as long as I could with one breath.

WAITING FOR SOMEONE TO LOOK AT ME AND SAY, "WHAT'S WRONG" (THEN I BLACK OUT, REMEMBERING NOTHING)

The people who hate you are strong when you misstep.

I can stand completely still.

I can never move again.

I will become the last warm blood cell in the not-breathing and useless you.

Teach me to trace the shape of the last warm blood cell in the not-breathing and useless you.

Teach me to stretch the last warm blood cell over my head and sleep on the ozone layer using my hands as pillows.

Am a good boy.

Am sitting in an alley behind a grocery store eating an apple and I don't believe anything.

If you touch my face you will know exactly what I look like.

Am your hero.

I like pineapple juice and I also like snowflakes.

No one is my hero.

A broken pencil in a two-inch puddle is my hero.

The broken pencil in the two-inch puddle stands completely still.

Am the broken pencil.

"SUCKS ASS" WOULD BE A FUNNY WAY TO DESCRIBE SOMEONE'S HAIRCUT IF ASKED FOR AN OPINION

I should wear a nametag everywhere I go—it would remove one more thing I have to say.

I don't laugh at anything anymore.

Someone stole my carbon copy and is making it do dumb shit.

And I'm just watching, laughing.

I LIKE WHEN SOMEONE ELSE SCRATCHES MY CHEST

I have copies of your dental record and I cover my window with them so your teeth and their roots are the first thing to touch my face when I wake up.

My face hurts from frowning.

And my hands are swollen from getting mad then doing nothing but sitting on them.

I am walking around and pushing the buildings of Chicago into Lake Michigan.

Would you be sad to see the building you're in become a boat. No you wouldn't.

I spend too much time worrying.

But I feel close to accomplishing the greatest feat of human quietness. I'm so close.

There is so much time I think I will prove it by doing nothing today.

Honestly, I am worried about falling in the shower.

Honestly, worried can be a nice feeling.

Honestly, somewhere in a cave there is a drop falling off a stalactite and it is looking around to see if anyone saw what it just did.

I am always trying to prove that I'm not a waste of time.

And if you smile, I win.

There is nothing that will still hurt my feelings. Nope.

My eyes float up and split in half along the sockets and I sit eyeless, seeing things I can't touch.

Best friends are flimsy.

I am not interested in being a good-looking human anymore.

If you smile I'm a good-looking human.

I win.

SCREAMING FACE

I saw a man fall while he was trying to get into his friend's car. He lifted his arm up and it was broken. It looked like he was screaming but for some reason I couldn't hear any screaming. He made a screaming face and his friend helped him up. The friend kept trying to put his coat over the man with the broken arm. It seemed like the friend was trying to make the man with the broken arm disappear into the coat. I would like to be able to make people disappear into my coat, but I wouldn't know where to start. True. It's like I'm always making a screaming face.

SOME SHIT ABOUT WHAT I'D DO WITH TIME TRAVEL

I'd go to the date of my death and take of picture of my face right before I died and then frame it and go back to the present and stare at the picture.

I'd go to my grave in the future and just sit there until I died, to confuse people.

And right now I am sitting and looking at the wall, drinking a glass of water and staring, and I don't ever think I am better than anyone else.

Not ever.

DON'T CONFUSE THE MARCH OF THE THING YOU HATE FOR HOW IT BLINKS ITS EYES AT YOU

When I grow up I want to be a fireman. When I grow up I want to be my own family. When I grow up I want to die. When I grow up I want to be left alone. When I grow up I want to be asleep on the floor of an empty apartment. When I grow up I want to have accomplished my present goal of distancing myself from everyone I know. When I grow up there will be no one who remembers anything about me. When I grow up I will barely remember anything about me and I will remember lying in bed guessing when the next lightning bolt will light up my room and show me I cared about this at one point but could never care again. Maybe that. When I grow up I want to be a middle aged man who people pity when they see him walking around, looking tired and ugly and never nice enough to want to get to know. Maybe that.

UNTITLED

The engraving on a nickel or dime or any coin should be someone sleeping on a couch with his/her winter jacket over him/her like a blanket, trying to avoid what comes through the blinds.

BECAUSE YOU KNOW YOU'RE AVOIDING GOING SOMEWHERE BUT YOU DON'T EVEN KNOW WHERE YET

Every person is an only child.

Practice how to discontinue your siblings.

I avoid entering my apartment if I know someone else is looking because I'm paranoid about people knowing where to find me.

But seriously, how are you today.

I got ok force and I use it on myself.

It takes a long time to patiently drop water onto a napkin one drop at a time so all the drops touch sides but it's worth it to create that kind of togetherness. It's worth it.

Right now you are looking at something that at some point I looked at and we are not going to die at the same time probably but the space in between deaths will be small compared to all known time and the idea of time in general.

The downside of smiling is smelling your own body cavity—the infected tissue inside on vacation that gives you a few decades of movement.

And if I reacted to other people the same way I react to myself I wouldn't have any friends.

I don't have any friends now but it's for different reasons I think.

In the morning when I'm hard, I don't think about anything while I wait to get soft.

I wait to get soft.

THE QUICK VERSION OF HOW TO BE SUCCESSFUL

Find a small place no one else can find.

THE INTRUDERS ARE REAL AND THEY ARE GOING TO KILL ME IF I STOP PROTECTING MYSELF

I sleep with my sheet wrapped all the way over my head except for my mouth because I am convinced the intruders will kill me if I see them.

I get sweaty when I am sleeping but being sweaty is better than getting killed by the intruders.

I sleep so they can't kill me.

But I won't yell if they do.

I don't know what I am doing but lately I have noticed that I don't listen to the first couple of words people say to me and then I have to like, catch up so I can understand them and reply.

Inside a big lake is a smaller lake.

Insider me is a bigger me.

Inside me is a much much smaller me that acts like it's huge.

And when your body shakes and the air in front of you says nothing and there is no one to confirm that you still make a difference, you will reach into your chest and the dust and crumbs will greet you.

LOVE STORY

I went to the gas station tonight to buy a drink. I had to wait behind a girl filling up her cup at the fountain. She sipped some of the drink and put a lid on it. I said, "If you were my girl, I'd buy you the 36oz. size fountain drink. You could have it all. You could have the biggest fountain drink in the world. We could die in it." She sipped her 22oz. sized drink and looked at me and said nothing. Then she walked away and I wondered what went wrong because I knew I pronounced everything right. It is hard to pronounce things right.

DEATH

I want to say, "Them's fighting word" to someone after they ask me what time it is.

My whole life is that feeling you get when you are at someone's house and you have nothing left to say—you have only been repeating things that already happened.

I keep a chart of the times I have accomplished complete silence.

When I walk down the detergent aisle at the store I can't breathe and I get drastic, looking around for help.

I will not make you feel ugly I will show you how fun it is to be a human. And how to not-want to be anything anymore.

Good.

IN THE LAST TWO YEARS I HAVE TALKED TO ANIMALS OR MYSELF MORE THAN I HAVE TALKED TO OTHER HUMANS

There is enough blood in my body to flood a dollhouse or at least fill up an average sized sock.

Tie your hands to your feet and lick your own genitals.

You can reward yourself.

We are going to be friends or enemies—I don't have neutral engagements.

To begin, melt your relatives and nationality.

Melt your fucking nationality.

I would like it if someone put me in a cardboard box and then taped the cardboard box up tight and lit the box on fire, kicking the box repeatedly.

Make me a dot-to-dot of your sudden dislike of my voice.

And make sure you do as little to help out other people as you can.

Make up a name for yourself.

And make up everything you ever tell anyone.

Your sweaty armpits are my pillows.

I scratch my face in your sharp, three day un-shaven armpits and feel drug-empty.

My sperm have misshapen heads.

And I don't contribute anything. True.

Being worthless is hard work, but you love everything about me.

Puzzles are shitty because you only end up putting together a picture that's already completed on the front of the box.

When I'm spending time with other people, I can only think about the moment when I'll get up to leave and how it will be signaled.

And yes, being asleep is fine, but it always ends.

And yes, sleep is fine but I'll stick with staying inside and looking out the backdoor or looking out the peephole at the hallways, wondering where all the people are going and why they aren't asking me to come with.

WHAT IT IS, MOTHERFUCKERS

The earth goes bald of all humans.
And it is impossible not to become a tradition.

I HAVE A PROBLEM WITH RANDOM LAUGHING

The weapon in your hand is more important than your hand or your heart or your head.

I want you to make me so upset I pass out. Then take turns.

I am aiming at the weapon in your hand, not your hand or your head or your heart.

Hold me and I will aim at myself. And then take turns.

We make a great team because you need someone to not-look at and I like to feel needed.

My spine is strong from holding up a huge hologram of pure shit.

YOUR EMBRYO

Break your embryo open and drink from it.

I pushed your face into the fabric of the couch and said, "I love you."

You looked one-day dead.

You smelled newborn.

We blended our cells together then ended.

I forcefed you smegma with my fingernail and we sat naked on the tile floor—carefully avoiding every emotion.

We became normal again.

I told you I was afraid to sleep because my dreams reproduced real life.

And I knew you weren't listening, so I said:

Everyone hates you and it is perpetual day.

Everyone hates you. It is perpetual day.

Everyone hates you.

Everyone hates you during perpetual day.

It is perpetual day and everyone hates you.

It is perpetual day and everyone hates you today.

Don't be afraid of sleep. Carefully avoid every emotion.

It is today and everyone hates you.

It is today and everyone hates you today.

It is perpetual day.

Break your embryo open and drink what is inside.

You will never recover from how you treat yourself.

And personality is something that is gone when you start talking.

My body leaves its outline on the ground forever.

Carefully avoid every emotion. Everyone hates you.

BIPOLAR IDIOT

And you will define yourself by hating your surroundings and hoping it's mutual so you don't look petty.

Standing directly in front of someone is a way to become the surroundings.

I pray you embarrass your enemies.

The less you say the more cleanly you die off this earth.

You become surroundings.

DICKHOLE

Being dead is the new alive.

I pulled my arm off and sharpened the bone and cut the earth in half and slept between the halves.

And volcanoes will return my blood.

And all earth is the hardened form of the dead-me.

And all earth controls the still-alive.

Sometimes when people talk to me, I feel like I just hit the garage door button and I need to run quickly to get out.

When you're sleeping, I put my fingers on your face and smear it around like a finger-painting.

But I make sure I put it back together the right way before you wake up.

My fun lasts forever.

An entire bottle of perfume washes my face.

Natural causes, they will not kill me.

My fun lasts forever in weakening approximations behind

old cells.

If you tell me you love me, I will keep saying, "What?" and acting like I genuinely didn't hear you until you hate me.

And that will be fast.

Burn your photo albums. They don't know you.

Today I am broken in half, staring up at the sky that raised me and it is bruised and split, spilling into my mouth, which I try to keep closed.

I want to cut your belly open and dip my feet in, like someone relaxing at the pool, on vacation.

But who knows.

Who knows how I will vacate.

Being alive on earth makes me feel like a spoiled kid at a sleepover at someone else's house.

WANTING OTHER PEOPLE TO THINK LIKE YOU IS DUMB

Two people were murdered outside my apartment last night. I think I would like the job of taking names off mailboxes. Or throwing the ashes of cremated strangers into the air. I think I would like the job of not remembering anything. Or trying to help other people forget things. I be tired as a motherfucker, that is true.

I'M NOT GOING TO CHANGE MY CLOTHES TODAY

I'm not going to change my clothes today.

I'm not going to be upset about eating by myself—I'm going to anticipate it positively.

I'm not going to change my clothes today.

I'm going anywhere today except for the bathroom and maybe even then I will stay there.

I'm not going to be surprised by anything.

I'm not big enough to control myself at all times—I'm small enough to hate every time I forget.

I'm not going to share anything.

I'm not going to fill up a brown paperbag with water because I know that won't work.

I'm not going to fill up a brown paperbag with water because there has to be a better way to build a friend.

I'm not going to change my clothes today.

I'm not going to allow myself the same kindness I allow others.

I'm not going to turn the lights on in my apartment from now on because I don't want to accidentally highlight my grave.

I'm not breathing I'm trying to inside-out myself.

I'm not going to change my clothes ever.

I'm not going to ask anyone how they're feeling.

I'm not going to change my clothes today.

I'm not going to lie, I feel like I need to become inside-out and touch the air as an inside-out person.

I'm not going to change my clothes today and I'm the material representation of an asshole that is six feet tall.

I don't know what time it is but I do know I'm not going to change my clothes today.

And I don't know what I'm doing.

You can borrow my socks if your feet are cold or if you just want to own something.

I'm not going to change my clothes today.

I SUCK

And maybe I get somewhere but my movement is decided by wanting to go, not wanting to go somewhere.

There are only small episodes where I can go without thinking about what I'm doing and how it is clearly not supposed to be like this. And that it will never end.

I have nervous rituals that only carry significance when I perform them alone. They are important to me.

Is it ok to sometimes see your own hands and jump back because you're worried someone is trying to choke you.

Guess what, it's too late, we're friends. And, something else, I can't remember.

And you will miss me, I know it. I know it.

HEY, MOLE ON THE LOWER BACK/ UPPER ASSCHEEK OF THE GIRL STANDING IN FRONT OF ME AT THE POST OFFICE

Mole On The Lower Back/Upper Asscheek Of The Girl Standing In Front Of Me At The Post Office, how are you.

I want to marry you. Just you, Mole On The Lower Back/ Upper Asscheek Of The Girl Standing In Front Of Me At The Post Office.

You are perfect.

Mole On The Lower Back/Upper Asscheek Of The Girl Standing In Front Of Me At The Post Office, do you need someone to look at you. I can do that. That's all I can do.

Make me a happy person. We are too right for each other to have to share. We shouldn't share.

I don't want many friends because I am too weak for that kind of work. I am too weak to have friends.

Mole On The Lower Back/Upper Asscheek Of The Girl Standing In Front Of Me At The Post Office, how are you— marry me, and I will break my fingers off using my bedroom door—make them into coins you can redeem for kisses.

And the kisses will make me weak.

Mole On The Lower Back/Upper Asscheek Of The Girl Standing In Front Of Me At The Post Office, stay with me.

NO TOLERANCE

I catch the flies on your corpse and take the blood back from each and rebuild you because I want to apologize for wasting the years you thought could've been used to do something even though I know you are wrong.

FOUR APOLOGIES

This is an apology to my roommate. You're right. I should've first asked you if you wanted an "artic adventure." And I should've explained that an "artic adventure" is when I dump a bunch of snow on you while you're sleeping. But we need to resolve this. Because someone needs to cook dinner for you and then not hear the words "thank you" even though they're so easy to say.

This is an apology to the comic book character on my underwear when I was five. I am sorry for shitting on a likeness of you when I was in kindergarten. I didn't know I had the flu. If I had known, I would've worn my striped underwear.

This is an apology to my bathroom floormat. I am sorry. I didn't know I'd become too destroyed to want to leave my apartment and wash you. If it's ok with you, I think I will fold you twice and then put you behind the toilet and forget about you.

This is an apology to the cat I saw smashed in the road. I couldn't remember how to perform cpr on a dead cat. Plus I didn't want to have to dodge cars.

HEY LEG-PINCHER, HOP ON MY BACK, I'M HORNY-NICE RIGHT NOW

We don't have anything in common.

FOR SOME THINGS, THERE IS NO ERASER

I can't help but think of how disgusted people must feel when I give them a hug.

And compliments are filth.

We should wash each other and suck the soap from the ends of each other's hair—put our hands in between the folds of each other's legs—hug to keep warm—and dry each other with gauze pulled from the skinny space that divides thinking something and saying something.

I am convinced that aside from my room, no other place exists.

But I'm not lost because I'm not looking to go anywhere.

I think about pushing everyone I meet.

Or making cookies for them and then coughing onto the cookies before I bring them over.

Or making my blood into ice cubes and mixing them a drink.

Or sometimes I don't think about anything and I just wait for the person to leave.

You get used-to things not working, but never the ways they stop working.

FEELING LIKE SHIT WAS AROUND BEFORE HUMAN BEINGS

Sometimes I put my hand in my pocket and find little stones and pieces of paper and I hold it all in my hand and say, "What happened to me" and I try to remember my multiplication tables to show that I am still a good person.

DON'T BE A DICK, LOVE ME

If you ever buy a pair of pants that have big enough pockets, please let me live with my head in your pocket.

I would be able to keep your leg warm with my laughing.

I would be able to tell you when your phone rings or whether or not you have enough change to buy certain things.

Get some pants that have big enough pockets please.

Sew them on if you have to I guess please.

At first it will be hard for you to walk with my head in your pocket, clinging to your leg.

But you will get used to it.

You will do anything for me I guess please.

Pull out your hair on a sleepwalk and stick it to the wall by the dead root ends I guess please.

Wait.

IT IS WEIRD TO BE AT A HOUSEPARTY WHERE EVERYONE IS ALIVE EXCEPT YOU

Every time I blink I'm worried everything else will die.

"Soft and shiny" is a good way to describe your hair after using some really good shampoo.

"Soft and shiny" is also a good way to describe a really old apple that is growing a beard of glitter.

Somebody just kill me already.

Email me and I'll give you my address and I'll leave my doors unlocked.

I'll even leave a big rock by my bed with a note by it that says, "Keep going, you're almost there!"

Yesterday, I put butter knives in my mouth and acted like a walrus. I wish someone was around to see it.

And the message is always the same.

I'm not trying to solve anything or help in any way.

The message is always the same.

FUCK YOU, DUMMY

My uvula is a birdcage trapping a scared, dying bird.

And loneliness is the reward for not wanting to contaminate someone else's life.

You can re-create the entire material world with a dot-to-dot.

Except for the paper where you diagram the dot-to-dot.

I BELIEVE IT'S OK TO PERMANENTLY DISFIGURE YOURSELF

Someone else usually says what I am thinking before I convince myself that no one else is thinking it or would ever think it.

I bought a small gift and wrapped it and hid it in my closet.

I found the small gift three months later and got really excited.

It was like someone cared about me.

It was like I convinced myself someone was thinking of me or would ever think of me.

Every day, I open the door to my closet and grab my coat then put on my coat and pause and think about getting into the closet and sitting down and shutting the door.

The only reason I don't do it sometimes is because I am worried I won't be able to find the doorknob again.

Things like that are scary.

And guess what, I'm fucking cool.

I recommend you treat the public like your own birthday party.

EVERYTHING IS A CALENDAR

Whenever I eat an apple I put the sticker on my shirt, and sometimes in the morning when I go to put on a shirt I notice a large collection of stickers and that's how I know how old I am. Yep.

AT A RESTAURANT I SAW A GUY WITH A LONG-ASS BEARD (NO, NOT LONG ASS-BEARD)

1. At a restaurant I saw a man with a very long beard. I said, "I like your beard." He said thanks. Then I said, "We should be friends."

2. At a restaurant I saw a man with a very long beard. I said, "I like your beard." He said thanks. Then I interlocked my fingers and put my thumbs together and said, "What do I have to do to walk away with that bad-boy in my pocket."

3. At a restaurant I saw a man with a very long beard. I said, "I like your beard." He said thanks. Then I said, "If I were riding you like a horse, I would hold onto you with both hands on either side of your beard." He said, "That's the only way to do it."

4. At a restaurant I saw a man with a very long beard. I said, "I like your beard." He said thanks. Then I said, "When it gets heavy with ideas, what do you do." He said, "I always shake it out before I enter my house." I nodded and said, "Ah."

5. At a restaurant I saw a man with a very long beard. I said, "I like your beard." He said thanks. Then I said, "If you're good today you can come over and I'll comb it and sing you

a song." He said, "I'd like that."

6. Today at a restaurant I didn't talk to or look at anyone and I called myself boss.

IS VERY DIFFICULT TO UNDERSTAND WHAT OTHER PEOPLE THINK (IS VERY DIFFICULT)

Most of my day consists of attempting not to be noticed by people.

Sometimes when I notice someone looking at me, I say, "We can act like this never happened."

There is no afterlife. The afterlife is people taking turns telling you how stupid you are, without end.

I hate it when you put your arm over me while we're sleeping because it prevents me from getting up and running away as fast as I can.

Plus it makes me sweaty.

Plus I can't stop thinking about biting your arm really hard and seeing how long it takes you to wake up.

Plus you are a dead body.

Plus I hate being touched.

Plus I hate.

Priceless. Dying of cancer times a billion.

Is normal to never have fun. People who need to have fun hate themselves and are afraid to die.

Is fun to wash my entire body with napkins. I wet with sink water then lie down on my couch feeling sorry for myself. Is very fun.

And now I will slowly breathe out the same air I was going to use to call myself a real motherfucker.

A real motherfucker is designed to produce real motherfuckers.

When you see someone you want to say hi to coming down the sidewalk, hide behind something then jump out and say hi.

Is very difficult not to become the entire world. Is very difficult.

Hi.

EARLIER I THOUGHT, "CUT A BIG WOUND INTO YOUR CHEST, IT'LL BE OK"

I found a turtle on the side of the street today. When I bent down to look, its head went into its shell. I said, "I know what you mean."

If I was a miniature farmer farming the carpet in my apartment, I would make a scythe out of a toenail clipping and a pretzel rod.

I don't know what I'm doing and I'm a dummy though.

And uh, the only way to bring something back to life is to leave it alone.

I wish there was a cord attached to my forehead that I could pull to raise my skull like a collapsible puppet.

What moves tree branches—is what sends a dead leaf out into the middle of a large puddle—is what pushes a flimsy moth into flight—is what in haphazard precision parts your hair—is what comes from where you can't see and calms your terror-face while you're trying to sleep—is what I eat and blow out into your face when I am on top of you or you are on top of me—is what will outlive us all—is nothing to be proud of.

This sucks.

A world of love would implode just as quickly as a world of hate.

Not everyone can be loved.

You are not important.

After I cut notches into your skeleton and climb to the top, I get to the top and feel cheated.

After I get to the top, I get to the top and I feel cheated and I will drop a rock and listen for it, to measure the height.

I WANT TO SCREAM IN SOMEONE'S FACE AND INTIMIDATE HIM/HER

It is the end when you don't want to trouble the only person who will still help you—when you are to them what you are to yourself.

It is the end when you are too stupid to move.

The tail of a dead animal in the street still moves because there is wind, not because it is still alive.

NEANDERTHAL CLITORIS

The worst position to be in is to have someone care about you more than you care about yourself.

The worst position to be in is to be that person.

The worst position is to be a person.

Everyone needs to hate someone else.

Being that someone else is as good a goal as any.

You are my favorite failure and I am too destroyed to get off the couch—I guess I'll sleep on the couch without brushing my teeth.

Everyone needs to hate being a sleepy failure with a goal but I want to be buried in a coffin—holding another human who died on the same day as me, both of us wearing crowns made of construction paper with plastic jewels glued on.

Ouch, this is hurting me.

Ouch.

The worst position is the one you began with and then continued to make worse.

I LIKE WHEN A GIRL HAS PAINTED NAILS/TOE-NAILS

The fly won't make it across the highway because there is so much wind and none of it moves in the same direction.

None of it moves in the same direction and nothing gets me hard anymore.

Some things are so pretty when I look at them I fear a stroke or some kind of instant death. Some things are so pretty I fucking hate them.

There is a part of me that intensely hates the sink in my bathroom. There is another part of me that thinks I just haven't gotten to know the sink in my bathroom well enough.

It will be easy to tape our hands to each other's heads, we just have to stay still.

It will be easy to get through this, we just have to stay still.

I am sitting on the sidewalk alone, brushing the sidewalk with an old leaf and I hope a plane falls on me.

Around the age of my death I won't remember today at all.

I have forgotten nearly everything that has ever happened to me.

The crumbs on my bed fill my mouth. I blow them up into my ceiling fan and watch where they land. But I don't really care where they land because I will find them again and I will pick them all up again.

Involvement with other humans is difficult but sometimes people let you steal their better qualities if you can convince them those qualities are ugly.

And then um, you become a saint.

I DAYDREAM ABOUT MY HANDS BECOMING LIQUID

Money is stupid.

My mind is ruined.

Most peoples' parents make me intensely uncomfortable.

SILENT DINNERS FUCKING RULE

Don't wake up ever.

The indentation above you upper lip is my crib and I am never going to wake up and I won't be fun to find.

I drew a circle on the wall and I tell time by how my head moves through it as a shadow when I sit in front of it.

It is stupid that I have clothes and places to be and I think I have a wallet somewhere and a lot of cups around my room and that's it—I think that's all I have—but it's still pretty stupid.

Part of me wants to light my apartment on fire and just sit there.

Part of me wants to light my apartment on fire and run.

And when I wake up in the crib that is the indent above your upper lip I use the pieces of the crib to build a rocket to the top of your head.

Uh if I knew what your favorite color was I would make everything that color, including myself.

It is time to regret everything.

It is time to leave my arms in the sun so they soften and then stretch them long enough to be able to gently set you down far away.

I leave my arms in the sun and they soften and I stretch them, but now I can't touch anything that is directly in front of me.

It is best to think about nice things while I eat you clean of your period.

You lose.

A LOT OF PEOPLE LIVE IN CHICAGO (I'D SAY, A SHITLOAD)

Tonight I went out to get food and when I paid, I said to the woman, "Keep the pennies." She told me to have a nice night. I took the food and ate it in the snow, sitting next to a bush and a garbage can. I decided that I would squeeze the legs together of the next nice person I met and then refuse to let go until maybe that person tried to attack me. I went to sip my drink but there was no straw in place. I looked for a straw but there was no straw. I decided the next nice person I encountered I'd pin down and appreciate. Sometimes I'm ruined.

I HAVE BAD URGES

There is no way to teach someone how to gently take apart a human life when that someone is the someone who taught you.

It is impossible not to want to do certain things.

And I saved everyone some time by feeling as unhappy as I could, unassisted.

I don't like it when the water gets cold around my ankles in the shower. I usually think, "Oh shit" and I look up at the ceiling like there might somehow be an escape.

You are my favorite person in the whole wide world though.

And I like myself. And I like you.

There is nothing you can do to kill me, so don't even touch me at all it makes me hate you that you think that's even possible.

My sex organs ache, always.

TWO PEOPLE KICKING MY HEAD AT THE SAME TIME, ONE IN FRONT AND ONE BEHIND

I cut my lips up into little flaps and then run them over your face and say, "Stay still, this is called 'Painting the House I Will Never Own' and it will never be over."

Then I repeat the phrase, "It will never be over" while continuing to paint the house I will never own.

The bigger the hearts get the more my teeth scrape them when I put them into my mouth but I will force them down whole, I promise that.

Swallow them whole and feel them pass through my organs, slowly each.

It will never be over.

You deserve a long afterlife that consists of a single hug from someone whose face you never see.

And you deserve to push me out a window while I am talking about how pretty it is outside. Be like, "Why don't you get a better look" and then push me out the window. Or suggest my shoe is untied, then do it.

I am worried I can't do it myself.

I HAVE A BIG BUTT

When people are storms, stand under them.

And use them to help you grow plants that look pretty and smell pretty but bear little needles filled with poison—because they will only touch you when you're attractive and you'll only touch them when you know it will hurt.

Keep your eyes open on other people.

Hate other people.

WHEN I GO FOR WALKS I PURPOSELY BRUSH UP AGAINST BUSHES AND STREET SIGNS BECAUSE, I DON'T KNOW, IT JUST FEELS SO RIGHT

Your bloody crawl is a red carpet.

Popped cherry is lipstick.

And somehow your bedroom floor is my grave.

I am horny to be a dead bird, smashed in a drinking fountain at the park.

Make me feel uncomfortable about saying anything—this can be done by saying nothing.

I don't know what I'm doing.

Our hymen hangs flimsy with holes from hungry insects.

I eat our hymen with little zipper teeth.

The zipper teeth spread my gumlines and my attempts not to smile are disgusting.

Our hymen is my bathing suit—make me a pool with what

you wring out of your pretty long hair.

Our hymen is a cloth I wave to assert allegiance, not block the heat.

When we go on a picnic I spread your part of the blanket over a fire.

All pulses are such bullshit.

I am almost done.

Take yourself out of the best friend game without saying goodbye.

By not saying hi.

DON'T BE A STEREOTYPE (OR DO, I DON'T CARE)

I have made many mistakes, but I'm not upset.

Between the ground and the air there is a plane of pure indifference that is exactly as tall as me.

Underneath my feet is becoming soft.

I would like it if I was a centimeter tall, unknown to everyone.

First thing I'd do is lie down in the carpet and sleep for a whole day straight.

Look out, here comes 2:53 a.m. and I don't have a family resemblance to anything but the combined sounds all animals make to alert when they're hurt.

I must be a hundred miles tall because when I lie down and then get up I feel far from where I began—same thing when I lie down.

There is only one lesson. There is only one lesson.

If I figured out what I was doing, I'd stop doing it.

Some things explode without moving.

Show yourself how to explode without moving.

Awesome.

There is only one kind of hurt and it comes to you in varying degrees of prevalence and uh, the worst degree feels like nothing is happening at all.

Holy fucking shit.

Forever is an idea that people made up to feel sorry for themselves.

Get on with becoming tired.

Be a stereotype then jump out of hiding when people have forgotten you exist.

Get on with becoming a tired stereotype.

There are many ways to say what seems like a lie but is completely true.

You can't teach yourself how to play on a playground when there is no one else there.

And you can't learn anything when there are other people there.

REALLY BIG CARROT

I bought a really big carrot at the store and I sat on a bench at the park eating the really big carrot and there was a kid doing somersaults. He was wearing a watch that looked cool. I thought about telling him how cool his watch looked but he seemed busy. I thought, "He will never know how I feel about his watch." He said, "That's a really big carrot" and I nodded and he somersaulted away. He looked really dizzy. I bet I could've easily pushed him over. Let's see, what else.

PASSIVE DEATH ALL DAY LONG

It's weird how many people I don't know.

I enjoy taking my life for granted—if you're asking me to do that with you, then yes I will. Then yes.

Cut out a circle of black construction paper and yell into it when you're scared.

And call me a name only you know.

I bury you in a grave of red light.

And everyone in heaven is homeless.

There are some things that I actually know.

I know I want to come on your face from really far away.

And I know I don't feel bad when someone blames me for making a mistake.

If I had a mascot, it would be an unidentified dead body with some dirt on its face and one of its pockets turned inside out and maybe both arms mangled, wearing a fanny pack that is full of dried bruises, and a dented face with a ripped-eyelid not covering the eye anymore.

Or maybe my mascot would be a hair that fell to the ground and blew beneath the closet door.

Or maybe I don't know.

I don't know how to look at anything the right way.

It is difficult to find something to look at when you don't want to look at anything.

Oh yeah, I just want to pinch you until you cry.

And nothing is clean enough to touch me.

I enjoy taking my life for granted and if you are asking to do that with me, then yes.

Yes I will.

So set my skinny corpse on a swing at a playground and never talk to me again, like you want to.

Set my skinny corpse on a swing at the playground and leave it there and walk away.

Last night I stood in the drive-thru of a restaurant and stared at the camera and smiled and waved. I kept doing that until an employee came out. Then I ran. I hid behind a bush in the parking lot of a bank and rubbed my fingers in the mulch and smelled them and I didn't want to leave.

UNTITLED

Behind every face is an expressionless skull.

This is true about anybody.

I can't tell if I'm really interested in anything.

And look, I didn't know that if I grabbed your face while you were sleeping and tried that thing where you pull a tablecloth off a table without disturbing what's on top, that it would hurt that much. I'm just an idiot human.

Glue a knife to your tongue and lick my belly like a bitch.

THE NAP (PART 2)

This morning I realized I was eager for the mailman to come (so I could see another person (even though I am almost convinced my mailman hates me and is secretly planning to kill me (pretty sure she wants to steal my blood and take my blood away in a bag then throw the bag into a big hole and bury it (pretty sure I am going to take a nap this afternoon (pretty sure I hate life because it is one long nap that breaks in intervals of waking up to being a completely different person, never achieving any result because never feeling exactly the same))))).

This line right here is one I put in as a way to make a pause, and feel calm again, hope that's ok with you.

A CERTAIN AMOUNT OF SEX ACTUALLY FEELS BAD

With a piece of sidewalk nailed behind my face, I'd still find a way to lift my face.

With a piece of sidewalk nailed behind my face, nothing would change.

I'd still lift my face and keep it off the ground.

I'd still change nothing.

With two lives I'd use the first to figure out how to make the next one even worse.

Do you believe me.

We can meet in the corner of space where people forget to check—where I do things I have to do with my eyes closed.

The fifth orgasm rips the groin the bestest and I am a beautiful human.

I eat jewelry and give nothing in return.

And youth is the thing that keeps ending.

Unlikely future.

No one has to protect the animal with the big jaw from the cross-eyed palsy holding a bb gun.

The cross-eyed palsy holding a bb gun threatens nothing.

The ground will get cold soon and I'm waiting to be there, to freeze with it and be cold until the sun tries its best to get beneath and cook me.

I actually feel ill with how negative I have become.

But I don't have any negative feelings about the carpet in my apartment.

And I don't have any positive feelings about cleaning it.

I only have interest in continuing to rub my feet on it then sending electricity through my nose to my cat's nose to give my cat braindamage (hopefully (wink wink)).

All things keep ending.

Do you believe me.

YOU WILL NOT CELEBRATE

When you know all the words to some television commercials you will not celebrate.

GROSS BODY GETTING FED THROUGH A PINCHED-OPEN MOUTH

When I take my temperature it reads: "Fucking perfect."

Please take good care of my frozen ghost. Don't let it look at the sun.

Today a car drove by me and someone yelled, "Fucking human."

That face-down-on-the-couch-you-wouldn't-get-up-if-the-ghost-of-the-previous-decade-called-from-the-hallway kind of tired. That kind. You know.

God bless America. There is so much of my semen on your bedspread you will never forget me.

I am having hurt insides all the time. But that doesn't matter.

I am convinced I don't have actual organs.

There are only bags of water inside me.

Winners are always violent.

Winners are always looking for more losers, because people only lose once.

Maybe I am full of shit.

Yes, I am full of shit.

But sometimes I accidentally tell the truth.

And everything kills everything else.

I wish there was a really small room in your house that I could live in and never leave. I'd get thinner and thinner but never die. You'd check every once in a while to see if I was still there and every time I'd say, "hi" and probably nothing else.

Everything else.

GETTING SHOT IN THE EYE WITH AN ARROW PROBABLY WON'T EVER HAPPEN TO ME (FINGERS CROSSED)

The ideal place at someone else's house is kneeling with your face stuck between the cushions of a couch.

I am most afraid of forgetting how to do things and then being embarrassed when I can't do them in front of others like I said I could.

It is impossible to inhale water without hurting your chest.

Maybe I am floating above a tree that is on fire, breathing in the smoke and maybe I like who you are but it is difficult to figure out what to do with my hands when a lot of people are looking.

There are little rocks in my urethra and I paint each one with a nontoxic marker and fill a cartridge with them then shoot myself in the chest and call it a constellation.

The whole world shares the same memory bank.

Forgive the people who would die without your forgiveness but do it right after they have almost died.

UNTITLED II

I wonder if doctors that deliver babies ever do a trick similar to that "quarter in your ear" trick except with like, a nerf football soaked in fake-blood. Everything I do is proof I didn't do the thing before it well enough. Get over this. You can do it.

THE LAST TIME I SAID SOMETHING RACIST, IT WAS UNINTENTIONAL, I WAS IN SECOND GRADE AND I MADE MY (FIRST) MEXICAN GIRLFRIEND CRY AND IT SUCKED

A sleeping bag at the bottom of a lake is my preferred afterlife just so you know in case you're in charge.

Today after you leave I nail boards over the door.

If you try to come back before I have the boards all the way nailed up then I nail you to the wall and walk away and never come back.

I can solve anything.

We can halt our debts if you just admit I am better than everyone else, at everything else.

I SAW FLIES ALL OVER MY ROOM LAST NIGHT AND I WASN'T ON DRUGS

There is no name for the color of your cheeks when you are hurt and halfdead and wishing you could float away, eyes closed.

There is nothing prettier than the color of your cheeks when you are too hurt to speak, wishing I'd float away, eyes closed.

There is no way I will ever float away because I am too heavy right where I am and there is no way you will float away because I am your orbit.

Yeah I'm your orbit.

Ugly girls make me harder than pretty girls yeah.

And yeah I have on a sweater that needs to be washed yep.

I feel good because I stopped trying to be a human yep.

I had sex two nights ago but I am so alone yep.

I can make anyone's life better than my own by simply staying away.

Lightbulbs holding different colored ink make my body cavity move and I hope they don't break I guess yep.

When your cold hand is under my shirt on my back I am even less human than usual.

That should hurt your feelings.

When I come in my sleep uh the whole world is deflowered.

I go to the bathroom and wash my hands clean of the smell of your hair and then I am weightless.

That should hurt your feelings.

My self-tracing daydreams remind me of myself ouch.

That should hurt my feelings.

I feel like something ended a long time ago and I can't figure out what happened but I know it's important.

My life will end prematurely yep.

I forget a lot of people without even trying.

That should hurt feelings.

There is no name for that color, but I think about it as I'm floating away halfdead, eyes-closed.

SOME PEOPLE DESERVE TO BE TREATED POORLY

I like to know when a kiss is coming; I don't like to be surprised.

I identify with pieces of spiral notebook paper that get ripped out but, like, split down the side all crappily.

The transformation from sleepy to more sleepy is always, and I am only good at getting thrown into bigger piles of things that don't work.

You can always change my mind though.

And I can always get along with anyone.

Some people deserve to be treated poorly though.

They will announce themselves though.

CRUSHING IRRITATION (OUTSIDE I FEEL UGLY)

A grave for a string is a straight line.

A grave for anything else is the shape of that anything else.

There is nothing wrong with being a fucking failure.

It takes more than one person to make a fucking failure.

I want to thread my face with wire and hang from my face until I pass out.

There will never be new sounds.

I can't imagine the task of remaining completely still.

I teach a space how much it holds by filling it.

I invented the colors and lines that make up a confused face.

Not going to fail at anything ever—that's how I feel.

And the purest moment of panic is when everything is right.

I wouldn't be surprised if I put my hand on the back of my head and it just went through my face without feeling anything and uh yes your ghost lives off the sweat from my sleeping forehead, so there.

You can bother others by just sitting still.

And yes a grave for a human is a skull.

And yes I will start an orphanage by abandoning myself.

My eulogy will be "sometimes nice but sometimes an asshole" or "sometimes had feelings" or "always shared" or "always worried about things that never happened."

THE GUM ON THE FLOOR IS ME (IS ME ON THE FLOOR)

Last night I was ordering a sandwich and the employee asked me if I wanted the sandwich toasted. I pointed my finger at the employee's face and said, "One day, everything will be toasted, and you will be the first, sweetheart." When I filled my fountain drink, the flavor was empty; it was just seltzer water. I took one sip and set the drink down and walked away. I walked away thinking, "There is nowhere far enough to walk."

THE APOCALYPSE HAPPENS EVERY TIME SOMEONE DIES

The worst part about being alive is thinking about it.

I farm gravedirt.

Today I was sitting in a chair at a restaurant eating and I felt a little hand on my head and I turned around and there was a woman holding a baby and the woman said, "He just wants to touch your head" and I said, "That's fine" and then the baby laughed and slapped my head a little bit.

I wish I were my girlfriend because then I wouldn't exist or at least I could act like I didn't.

Is hard not to feel like my bed is a lake when you're so sleepy and blue-faced and heavy. Is hard.

I am hard right now and I smell terrible.

What's new with you.

Everyone is describing the same thing.

I am part of the thing being described.

Another part of the thing described is everyone describing it.

I want to break someone's jaw with my head. For real.

I think maybe I forgot to say hello at the beginning of this.

I'm real sorry.

WE ARE GOOD AT BECOMING OLDER

Being insecure is the best way to protect what you no longer want.

And every day I remember things that remind me I'm a brand new human every few seconds and every few seconds I'm reminded I'm always a brand new version of the same person—never different—reinvented every few seconds as the same aging pile of ridiculous garbage.

I am ok with that.

God bless my shapeless head.

At night my head deforms into dragonflies that collide with trees and eat their own wings to stay alive.

Real life is a low-moving wind in the shape of a scythe.

I am ok with that.

And everyone I meet loves me.

I win over so many hearts I need a bigger chest.

The best way to get older is to try not to.

So be happy.

Because I'm willing to build a treehouse in your backyard to protect you.

Can I come over and sit in your fridge.

What time will you come over and hammer me into the ground with your balled hand.

Fuck my birthday, but yeah.

No one trusts you if you think no one trusts you.

I HOPE I GIVE A CONVINCING THANK YOU TO SOMEONE BEFORE I DIE

There will always be something I can't tell someone else. And there will always be someone else who doesn't want to listen.

Sometimes I'm convinced that everything and everyone is an arrangement meant only for me to experience and that an afterlife is not something you bridge but experience through unending life.

And when you are surrounded by people who care about you, you will never hit the ground and that's a bad thing I guess, so what.

I have never heard a person say, "so what" unconvincingly.

I want to offer help to someone with his/her groceries then throw the groceries on the ground and bend myself into a crab-like stance, hissing at the person to make him/her think I feel threatened.

I own everything.

I can't believe I own everything.

A pie chart of the percentage of my time spent worrying

would be a monochromatic circle and I'd be able to draw it with my eyes closed.

If you move from worse to worse you will always have just been better.

It'd be nice to just knock on someone's door and hand them an apple. "Thought you might need this, you know, for whatever." Then smile and walk away, not looking back.

When I haven't clipped my toenails in a long time I get paranoid someone else will see them and accuse me of being an animal.

I wouldn't mind being killed and stuffed like an animal, but I would mind being treated like an animal you just hit with a shoe to expel from somewhere.

If someone hits me with his/her shoe, I would feel worthless.

So bad being the person that is this particular amount of experiences, thought about and remembered this particular way.

But there is no way to know whether or not I am jealous of anyone else.

Worried about trying to befriend everyone you meet, you be the shittiest person ever, sure.

Call me when you have some time.

BOO

Boo—I think you'll love rubbing our bellybuttons together to make them whistle.

Boo—I think you'll love trying this new thing.

Boo—I'll wear a paperbag over my head if you stab me repeatedly in the chest.

Boo—I'm going to handcuff you to yourself at seven years old.

Boo—I'm almost entirely convinced no one really likes me.

WHERE DOES GLITTER COME FROM, IS THERE LIKE, A MINE?

After I remove my nervous system, I stretch it over my lap and poke it repeatedly with a needle that I have not cleaned, the whole time singing a song that reverses my age.

And uh, you are always alone.

And for as many people as there are, it feels like there is only me.

At night I sit in a folding chair in my room.

Sometimes I just sit naked and look out the window.

I think about running and tripping face-first through the window.

If someone hugged me right now, the world would be solved.

Everything should be how I want it but I don't really care.

I just exploded and returned to form in one of tonight's many silences.

COPS FREAK ME OUT BECAUSE I DON'T LIKE WHEN PEOPLE TRY TO CONTROL ME

If you don't hate yourself, everybody else will.

And they will never do as good a job.

There is no one I wouldn't watch, to learn a new way.

You are my favorite though. You are the very best work.

26 years ago I was born when a waterlogged tree split in two and I stepped out exactly how I am now, 26 years old, already declining in new and wonderful ways.

ELDERLY COUPLE

Tonight I sat in a booth at a fast food restaurant and looked out the window and in the parking lot there was an elderly couple sitting in their car eating ice cream together and they looked so happy that I asked one of the employees to kill them for me but instead of complying, the employee asked me to leave. I waved to the elderly couple in the parking lot as I walked by. It's hard not to become an elderly couple yourself when the only person you talk to is yourself and you're so in love.

CAT SKULL

I like to put my hand beneath my pillow then pull it out, act like it's a surprise gift.

Frowns need friends too.

I guess I am the shittiest human ever, I guess.

I have become paranoid that people are mailing me nice letters saying how much they want to touch me and kiss me and comb my hair but the mailman is throwing the letters out just to cause pain in my life.

There are no new ways to make an enemy.

And no new ways to give a gift.

How are you going to leave.

Me, I plan on standing still and letting it pass, never acknowledging that what is hurting me is hurting me.

I WORSHIP SATAN

I'll breathe on the windows and trace a face that is mine and yours.

I'll rip your ear open with a secret.

The secret will turn to icicles stringing the torn canal.

Say hurray for the length of time you get to make things happen.

Say hurray, you fucking ingrate.

If you come to my apartment I will let you drink some of my blood and you won't even have to pay for it.

When we go on a picnic together I spread your part of the blanket over a hole that leads to the opposite side of the planet.

When I was rereading this, I saw the words "blanket" and "planet" and that made me think of a planet whose surface is all blankets.

And I loved the planet.

Hail satan!

He is good!

SELF-ESTEEM

I'm combing your hair with my fingers, you motherfuckers. And yep, the receipt for my kisses is a leaf stapled to your cheek and you feel blessed. Don't worry, I will not refuse to offer you a hammock in my heartvalve when you look really tired. And yep, I love myself. I get blisters in my throat from holding in all the nice things I want to tell myself. I love myself and yep I love my throat blisters, they are the receipts for the kisses I get from people I don't trust and it's hard not to become tired when everyone is the same.

HOLOGRAPHIC PERSONALITY DISGRACE

I'm only mean to you because I have a crush on you.

I'm not trying to hurt anyone's feelings uh I wish I could cup my hands around the blackest corner of my closet and bring it to you and say, "See this, do you understand."

Turn around real quick, you'll see the thing that was following you and you'll regret what it is but not that you saw it.

Sometimes I have to go to the bathroom or a private place when I'm in public so I can clench both of my fists and grind my teeth and kneel down and press my face against the ground until the energy goes away.

The energy is not my best friend.

I'm in a canoe inside one of your veins and when I get to your heart I am going to stretch out and then do a cartwheel and laugh loudly until all the laughs start ricocheting and I have to be careful I don't get caught in my own barrage.

Or some-shit.

Some people are just assholes.

Some people are such assholes that saying, "Look, again, I'm sorry I cut off my thumb and glued it to your baby's head because I thought you'd like him better as a unicorn" means nothing to them.

Some people are assholes.

And everyone must have a crush on me because I feel like shit.

RELATIONSHIP

I am waiting for you to make a mistake.

And I am certain you die in my lap, in that you are a matchstick on a glacier.

Forget the very small attempts to boost your esteem that have been made by people all your life because I am staring at your forehead and it owes me some time alone and I owe it a hole for the world to step in and clean their feet off before saying hi and staying over way too long.

ONE THING CAN EXPLAIN EVERYTHING ELSE

The sunshine left inside the skin gets microwaved out.

Blood cells left inside the muscle get made into perfume and make-up for our faces.

The frisbee upside down still holding very cold rain gets tipped over to prevent small animals from drinking.

The muscles that make our genitals get unwound and thrown upward and when they fall on our faces we laugh and thank the sky for deciding not to kill us just yet because we have so many more important things to do.

The things around us get made into things we want to have and we are the things around us.

I ALWAYS THINK, "IF I JUST GET A GOOD AMOUNT OF SLEEP I'LL BE FINE"

But I never seem to get the right amount of sleep.

Last night I came in my sleep, sleeping on my back with both arms pinned, and when I woke up, my room was a giant black cube funneling itself into my mouth and nose and I was afraid and I couldn't move my arms.

One day I will fulfill my greatest aspiration when I walk down the sidewalk and take off my pants and beneath the pants there will be another pair of pants and then I keep walking, never returning to retrieve the previous pair of pants.

And no one is going to cry when I'm dead.

I AVOID WASHING DISHES BECAUSE I USUALLY REMEMBER SOMETHING AWFUL IN THE SILENCE

The best position to be in is sitting on the couch with nowhere to be—or no, facedown on the couch with nowhere to be.

I wouldn't mind living another eighty years if I never had to see anyone again.

Or if someone mandated that I had to wash a stack of dishes that took me eighty years to finish.

The best position to be in is not knowing what the best position is.

LITTLE KIDS AND ANIMALS LIKE ME

I bought some sidewalk chalk and then I drew a person on the street and I feel asleep next to it—facing it—so I'd be the first thing it saw upon waking up, like I was the best thing ever (which I am).

I shaved off pieces of your heart and wallpapered my room with them.

And my head falls to pieces, which become headstones for the things I say I will do tomorrow.

PLEASE ADOPT ME

It should be illegal to look at another person without his/her permission.

My superpower is that I am a fucking asshole and I can't remember anything.

My superpower is that I only remember things that benefit me.

I want to sneak into your room and cut your mattress open and get inside your mattress so that only my face is showing.

Won't that be fun.

My face will be under your covers.

We can be friends and I can entertain you, to avoid feeling like a chore.

We can work out a system of bites and licks so if you ever roll over on me while you're sleeping, I can communicate that I am dying or that I just need to talk.

I wish cereal still made me excited.

Kill people by ignoring them.

And please please please, don't litter.

I LIKE TO HURT OTHER PEOPLES' FEELINGS SOMETIMES (I MEAN SOMETIMES IT ACTUALLY FEELS LIKE THE ONLY SKILL I POSSESS ABOVE ALL OTHERS)

When I wake up, I smell the clothes on my floor and whichever smells most like me I wear—otherwise I feel upset the whole day.

Just kidding, I always feel upset.

Just kidding, I'm good.

The number of shapes you can imagine in the atmosphere is infinite based on how small you imagine them and how long you keep trying.

Trying hard is the first step to being upset and not trying anything else for a while.

And getting to know something or someone is the first step towards harming it.

And someone will search my room hard for the remains of my shape.

Touchdown for me, you rat-bastards.

If life is a gift it's best to reject the gift, and not be greedy.

SELF-INFLICTED CONTRACEPTIVE IDEA

We fill a plastic shopping bag with dead bugs and study them in the bathtub.

And I admit that sometimes right after I wake up I stand on my bed and try to jump my head into the ceiling so my neck breaks.

Sometimes when you're not looking I take your shoes away from the front door and hide them so you think you have disappeared. And that is half true.

Sometimes I wear my shoes while I am sleeping because I'm worried the bad people will try to cut my toes off.

I like to sleep with pants on too so I can keep my hands in my pockets and feel safe.

If your jawbone fell off and mine did too, we could sleep upside down with our top teeth clenched. And it would be nice.

The window in my room is either what brings the entire world into my room or the thing that keeps the entire world out. And that is half true.

I never make a mistake.

Nobody is different and I think we should just agree to be the most important people in each others' lives because why not.

Every time I look at myself in the mirror on my showerdoor I look exactly the same. I always look so tired.

And since nobody is different, I am the most important person in my life.

And I never make a mistake.

COMMIT CRIMES/ KILL YOUR PARENTS/ LIGHT SOMETHING ON FIRE/ STEAL SOMETHING

Most of my day consists of attempting not to be noticed by other people.

Sometimes that involves jumping into bushes, or hiding beneath cars.

Sometimes that involves just smiling at someone.

It would require the biggest vacuum ever to take away my greatness.

So don't touch me.

Randomly asking someone if they are frightened is a good way to frighten them.

I like to take out a cellphone in public and pretend someone is on the other line. I like to say, "You bet your ass I want to dig out your tongue and suck the blood out of your screaming mouth, when are you available."

People are impressed when it seems like you have things to do.

The times I wake up and see a hair on my pillow, I think maybe you came over and lay down for a while and left, but usually it's just a stray armpit hair of mine—which makes me think about what you'd look like with a head full of armpit hairs—which makes me think I would like you so much more if all the hair on your head was armpit hair.

And things end when not given attention.

Be very upset when things end.

Be happy that things end.

Commit the greatest crimes by letting yourself end.

IDEALLY AT SOME POINT IN MY LIFE I'D LIKE TO EMERGE FROM AN ALLEY AND STAND IN FRONT OF PEOPLE ON THE STREET AND SAY, "REAL PAIN" WITHOUT LOOKING AT ANY OF THEM, THEN RETREAT BACK INTO THE ALLEY

People die.

Don't worry, people die.

Sometimes when I'm wiping my ass, I look at the toilet paper with the shit on it and I say, "People die" but I mean it more as an assurance.

You must be a mouse because I always find you frozen and scared on the kitchen floor.

You must be my best friend because it seems like you never existed.

We should buy an extra big pair of jeans and get into them together and do a cartwheel.

I am the only furniture in my apartment and vague disappointment is the only furniture in me.

I am the only furniture in my apartment and big disappointment is the only furniture in me.

FALLING ASLEEP ON THE COUCH = FAILURE

I wear gloves in the shower to make sure I don't accidentally touch myself.

Don't teach anything, except how to be a seizure of space.

I lick the cold water along the bottom of the kitchen sink when it's really late and I don't know what to do or if there is even anything to do.

Is easy to feel like my only option is to pull my hood over my head and duct-tape it shut and then roll around on the floor screaming.

Is very easy.

I don't recognize myself when I am talking to someone.

Myself, the only human alive.

My headstone will be a mirror.

The distance from me to another human is making my legs wobble.

But there is nothing I can do.

There is nothing to do but hide.

I want to be a vampire that only drinks blood out of your hip.

I will be a nice enough vampire to only drink enough blood each night to survive.

I won't like, go all out or anything, and totally kill you.

Because then I'd have to find a new person and a new hip and we have such a good relationship going anyway.

My superpower is that I can't deal with everyday situations without feeling like that last bit of semen that clogs my pisshole after I'm done fucking myself.

Uh, fuck yeah.

Is very easy.

I would be in a commercial for apple juice if someone asked me.

I hope that you live a long life of many nice moments, until you die, staring at the ceiling with the swaying light of the blinds projected, less nice than the sun but still very nice like something you might want to jump into.

No one needs to have their feelings hurt. No one deserves anything.

I hope we live to be a hundred so it takes us a hundred years to die. Is very easy.

PEOPLE WHO DO COCAINE ARE USUALLY FUCKHEAD DICK CULTURE

The back of my forehead feels very dirty.

THERE IS NO WAY TO WASTE TIME

The wires that control my mouth feel thin.

It has become hard to say things that make people nod.

Some people will only welcome you back when you are injured badly.

And what is sharp is mine to use.

I expect the same of you.

Clean the tools from yesterday.

Reach into the air and pull down your weapon and use it on me.

What is sharp I expect you to clean and use on me.

Make your pillow a small lake.

Make your teeth twenty-eight weapons.

Make your way to hell.

Make the earth shed the layers you step on, out of embarrassment at having your marks on its skin.

OXYGEN IS PRETTY GOOD

I don't have to accept anything about anyone.

And I feel like I am stupid looking when I smile.

If I could tape myself to your ceiling to become part of your life without you knowing it, I would.

If I could cut my tongue out and hide it in your room, I would.

If I could do a backflip, I would start a campfire and do a backflip into the campfire and try to just lay there.

Useless-pile type of gone.

If I could maintain lasting relationships with other humans and not feel like I was slowly getting my head ripped off by an invisible cloud, then I would probably maintain lasting relationships with other humans.

Useless-head type of gone.

Fog on, brother.

If I could tape myself to your ceiling and secretly become part of your life, I would leave my socks inside my shoes beneath me and then when you look up, I'd say, "You are so great it exploded me out of my shoes and now I am stuck on your ceiling, can I please stay."

But I'm at a point now where I honestly think I don't try at all to get people to like me, and it feels weird.

I DARE YOU NOT TO DIE WHEN I LICK THE BOTTOM OF YOUR FOOT WHILE WE'RE FUCKING

The thing about when someone dies is, they never expect anything from you again and you don't expect anything from them either.

That's the thing.

I hope I am not remembered by anyone.

Not having hope is not the same as being hopeless.

You're having fun, but it will end.

WHEN I MAKE A PEANUT BUTTER SANDWICH AND LOOK AT MY REFLECTION ON THE MICROWAVE I LAUGH AND SAY, "YOU SILLY MAN" THEN I EAT THE SANDWICH ALONE IN THE KITCHEN, LEANING MY BACK AGAINST THE COUNTERTOP

Me and you as small-enough to float on our backs in a puddle.

(Me and you hoping that the puddle is close enough to space to freeze)

Me and you shooting each other in the face at the exact same time.

(Me and you hoping we hit the ground at the same time, next to each other)

Me and you rubbing our assholes together.

(Me and you remaining good friends)

Me and you as a single body with two heads weighing down a struggling spine ready to peel.

(Me and you knowing we're too pretty for the stem)

Me and you with our backs broken, lying on the carpet in the living room not able to think of anything to say or even actual words.

(Me and you knowing we're the same thing)

Me and you being quiet

(Me and you and nothing else)

My high-fives turn arms to shreds.

And I don't feel embarrassed by anything anymore.

Right now I could get shot in the chest and stomach many times and not die.

Yowzers!

IN SIXTH GRADE I WATCHED THE JANITOR BEAT MY CLASSMATE AND I LAUGHED (OH HOW I LAUGHED)

A telemarketer called me today and I said, "Please don't hang up on me, please."

I can be confused for a napkin—skipping a playground at night—caught by a cold puddle and made too heavy to fly.

When you die I am going to use your body as a sleeping bag.

I rim my thoughts with gold and let them drop dead at the front of my mind before I say them—that's why I smile a lot.

I just want one friend whose sole job is to remember things I am likely to forget.

I pulled a scab off my knee and fed it to a bird.

And everyone loves me.

Cover the earth in mirrors and redirect the sun. And space melts in black streams and I open my mouth to each stream.

Each stream collects in deposits in my organs and makes my body fail.

I place myself in a drainage canal, lying down, completely still, without any emotion.

And you will not forgive me because I won't ask.

There is a pimple on my upper cheek, under my right eye, and it fucking hurts.

I cut down my family tree. I pulled up the trunk and broke each root in half. Laughter was the soundtrack. And tonight I will start a bonfire with the timber and stare at it until it answers my questions. I will put my head in the bonfire and keep my eyes open until they melt. Then I will put a small crab in each socket and hunt down all my idols with a saw in my hand.

Stay alive by not smiling, or, go fuck yourself.

I can be confused for my own ideal sex mate.

And everyone loves me.

COMPLEX NEUROTIC VISIONARY TORTURE

You are gum because you are useless after a few seconds and because when I take you out of my mouth and throw you into the street you get eaten by birds and it makes me laugh and I never think about you again. I think you could say the same about me.

"ASSWIPE" IS A GOOD WAY TO DESCRIBE SOME PEOPLE, OR MAYBE I AM WRONG

I saw my face in a puddle today. Then a twig fell from a tree and ruined the whole thing. When the puddle reformed, I saw my face again and thought, "Is that right."

Tic-tac-toe—I win every time because I always occupy the middle.

Tic-tac-toe—I am always in the middle.

Look how small my heart is.

I am a bug—am a rolled up newspaper.

I steal the wings off other bugs and throw the wings into the garbage.

And I wake up laughing a lot.

Sometimes I feel like my life is very empty and sometimes it feels too full to survive.

But I lose every time because there is no middle.

I DON'T WEAR TURTLE-NECK SHIRTS BECAUSE OF THE POWERLESS TERROR I EXPERIENCE WHEN MY HEAD GETS STUCK

The good thing about living in a tree is that you get no visitors.

At night I put my hand beneath a rock. I keep my hand cold underneath a rock all night and by morning you are the rock and your ass is my nylon mask and I am breathing eggs into you, and you say, "You destroyer you."

I wouldn't want to be a melting ice cube because I'd be afraid of not knowing where I was going.

Get no visitors.

Get home without looking at anyone.

There are folds in my skin that shake out the smoke from everything old and burnt.

I don't blame myself for falling asleep in one of the folds and giving up—because I'm old and burnt.

I don't blame myself for falling asleep.

And nobody belongs anywhere until they are old and burnt.

Until they get no visitors.

Until they get home without looking at anyone.

PAINLESS, WELL-WISHER EXTINCTION

I take big bites out of the sun and feel it expand in me.

And all feelings get eaten, and become stone, because they are small and worthless.

But they never erode, and today is the day I lie down on the floor and let the stones expand through my chest, snapping ribs upward into buildings that take big bites out of the sun.

I'M CONFUSED WHEN PEOPLE ASK, "WHAT ARE YOU GOING TO DO TODAY."

Hiding behind the bathroom door is one way to make your roommate uncomfortable (email me if you want the rest of the ways)

Filling a glove with blood and putting it in the freezer is one way to make a blood-hand popsicle (email me if you want the rest of the ways)

I get scared about dying when I remember that dying means you can't change anything anymore. But I can't even do that now so whatever. I will keep breathing until I try to breathe and I can't, and I just think, "This is ok."

SLOWLY NEGLECTING A RELATIONSHIP

Eternity in a combination-safe on the top of a mountain.

Uh huh.

Whenever someone says, "There are plenty of fish in the sea," I think, "There are many ways to boil the sea."

As a human, I am worthless.

As a thing that is quiet, I am best.

As a friend, I am both.

As the person who taped you to the bed last night because I was afraid you'd get away, I'm guilty.

As a person right now, I am hoping that someone poisoned the toast I made for breakfast and I just don't know about it yet but that it will kill me and put me to sleep on the floor of my bedroom underneath the ceiling fan, the one with the missing lightbulbs.

Fuck yeah, I feel better.

THERE IS NOTHING TO DO

Very unfair that I'm a human and not a stick.

HAVING A CELLPHONE MAKES ME FEEL CORNERED BUT I COULD SAY THE SAME THING ABOUT HAVING EYES TOO, I THINK

One time I fell off my bed while I was sleeping and hit my mouth on the ground and in the morning I woke up back in bed with my bloody lips stuck to the pillow.

It was bad having to pull my bloody lips off the pillow.

Something else, but I forgot.

And all I can do is shrug.

I stand in the corner of my room leaning my weight against my forehead pressed into the wall.

And I know I will fall down before the walls that are holding my head ever do.

I WONDER IF 'CLIVE JACKSON' IS THE NAME OF A REAL PERSON (IT HAS TO BE)

Hatred towards other humans is a form of infinite kindness.

I heart hatred towards other humans.

I heart anything that can't talk.

Realize you are more uncomfortable with yourself than anything else on earth.

Then understand why.

Then identify yourself in everything else.

Then never compare yourself again.

Usually, I don't realize the clothes I'm wearing are stained until I'm already out in public and it seems inexcusable.

I have let too many people embarrass me for it to ever happen again—I'm telling you.

There are burst capillaries where I pinch your legs.

I give you many gifts.

Not having anywhere to go.

I give that gift too.

You can come visit me but the way back is salt for shredded hands and knees.

I am having nowhere to go and it's a gift of mine, please come visit.

Your bone marrow makes my teeth bright. Your glass teeth break on my bones.

My birthday is May 26, 1983.

No repair.

I am curious as to how many paralyzed mice I could swallow whole before I'd feel sick and have to exhale their souls, in what I bet would look like green plumes.

No one but me sees the green plumes.

Tonight while I eat my dinner—sitting with cold feet on a couch that leaks white stuffing that attaches to my hair and stubble while I sleep—I will give each piece of furniture a name so the next time I talk to people I can tell them I was hanging out with objects that sounds like humans.

No repair. Countdown to being a green plume.Ending yourself while you're still young enough to be a gift.

LISTENING TO MY NEIGHBORS SCREAM WHILE I DO A PUZZLE

No one is here to help you, they're just afraid of what you'll do without any help.

This morning I ate a whole bottle of chewable multivitamins but I didn't become perfect like I thought I would, so I went back to bed.

I am wearing a bad-smelling shirt with a blue stain on it and I think it's from a pen—I need to become dead in your car real soon.

I love your ugly face.

I want to fuck you.

Drinking pine-scented floor cleaner will not get the demons out of you—it'll just make you have painful pine scented burps the next day.

Nothing is wrong, we just don't get along with each other.

Get your head off my lap, I have to piss. You wouldn't want me to piss on your head. Or if you would, then make that clear somehow, I don't want to make a mistake like that. I don't want to make a mistake like that.

I AM POSSESSED (NOT JOKING)

The stronger humans teach others to hate looking at their own bodies.

You'll never forget what I look like after I put my eyes close to your eyes.

When people say they wouldn't trade something for the world, they are being illogical because the world contains the thing they wouldn't give up.

Stay still while I bite a clump of hair out of your head—feeling horny about the clump's pressure stuck in my teeth. Because I am very in love with the things I don't remember well-enough.

I AM NOT UPSET

Eating a peanut butter and jelly sandwich for dinner like three or more times a week results in disappointment.

No actually that's selfish of me to think.

Push me over, I'm done.

Our time together will end with one of us hating what has happened.

Our time together will end and I won't apologize.

Our time together will end.

I GET UNCOMFORTABLE AROUND PEOPLE WHO GET ANGRY AT VIDEOGAMES

There is a place in my mouth that I have bitten three or four times today and now it is just long strings of pulp and it keeps getting stuck in my teeth and I'm trying to increase my courage to just swallow the pulp.

You are the person who colors your eyelids so people call you pretty when you cry.

I am the person who cuts pockets into my cheeks so the tears' salt thickens my face.

Love will heal the world.

I STILL HAVE ALL MY TEETH, HOMEY

Instead of a regular funeral, just duct-tape my body to a mattress and throw it into a forest preserve. I don't want to be any trouble.

Make up a symbol for your genocide. Some people will think it's nice without understanding it.

All of your relatives and friends are dying no matter how much you love them.

The same is true no matter how much you hate them.

At the age of 25, the bones of the human body fully harden, losing their pockets of air.

At the age of 26, I have become a pocket of air.

And I'm worried that there is a place bigger than earth, and that it will find me and I'll accidentally breathe it in, and that it will stay breathed-in—or that it has already happened and that's why I thought of what I just said.

Minus everything for me.

The air sews down what you leave behind in case you turn around and want to stay the same.

Trouble.

EXPRESSIONLESS DIGSUST IS MY NATIONALITY

If I bite you and all my teeth break out, I will thank you because you'll have shown me my teeth are bad.

Don't say thank you, it looks pathetic.

If you strangle me, your fingers will break on my neck. And I will thank you for reminding me. And you'll say thank you back.

I pick a tree out of the ground and stir the sky with it then put the tree in my mouth and see what it tastes like—but I don't tell anyone.

I need to find someone to buy walkie talkies with, and then go out into public and walk side by side saying, "Fuck you, over" back and forth.

THE BURGLAR

When I wake up and look around my room and remember everything about it and then decide to go back to sleep, it's the greatest feeling there is.

When I wake up on the couch and look around and decide it's time to go to my room, it's the greatest feeling there is.

When I am walking down the sidewalk or just sitting in the library and I remember that I will experience the same kind of days for millions of years, it's the greatest feeling there is and my dick leaks dirt.

You will find me and shake my hand when you realize what it means to be a purse filled with glass pulverized into dust—randomly combed by a small wind of self-hatred—and you will love me.

When I wake up, you will find me and shake my hand—having realized what it means to be a purse filled with glass pulverized into dust, randomly combed by a small wind of self-hatred—and you will love me.

I AM HERE

I am here and I just jumped to try to get away but earth pulled me back really fast and that makes me feel needed yeah.

I am here to secretly poke a hole in your leather couch so it loses value but you know nothing about it.

I am here to be an example of a washed-out fuck.

I am here to get high on my own bad mood.

I am here and the bugs bite my body while I am sleeping.

I am here and it makes everything feel like a terrible obligation.

I am here and I am pretending to sleep.

I am here to spend my life sharpening a knife that I use to cut my head off but then end up dying of old age a few inches into my neck.

I am here, and every time I think about it, I get grossed out.

Inner beauty is yours when I spit in your mouth.

SLEEPOVERS AT SOMEONE ELSE'S HOUSE ALWAYS SCARED ME WHEN I WAS YOUNGER BECAUSE I THOUGHT THE OTHER FAMILY WOULD SURROUND ME AND KILL ME

I bought you a balloon shaped like a star and I'm waiting until it barely floats before I give it to you.

There is nowhere else except for right here.

And everyone is trading air.

Sexual intercourse is here to stay, or some-shit.

You're an idiot if you want to play a role in anyone else's life.

You're an idiot if you think I won't glue your mouth shut and then open it by pressing my fingers in slowly.

You're an idiot if you approach the animal with the big jaw holding a toothbrush.

And the things you know will eventually be upsetting, are always the things you could never imagine being that upsetting.

Sexual intercourse is here to stay.

Don't get to know anyone.

Don't be ok.

Don't close your eyes to the long ladder of humans who you will never say hi to, and who will never say hi to you.

Don't go to sleep.

NOBODY CAN CONTROL ME

I am working towards making the walk to my grave the most unbearable and most solitary it can be.

And I don't feel sorry for myself.

I saw the words, "Happy birthday, Michael, we love you!" chalked on someone's driveway and it upset me for some reason.

I'm better than you at sitting still and looking at things.

I'm better than you at leaving my bed unmade.

I'm the best person ever at feeding goldfish, and smiling at babies.

So suck my dick I guess.

You wanted something from this piece of writing, but no, suck my dick.

PIECE OF WRITING THAT IS TONALLY DIFFERENT AND ENDS THE BOOK

Yesterday I realized home is the greatest enemy I will know.

Nothing can resolve the feeling that I am always far away from everything else and with every move I increase the distance.

And with me—with everyone—I realize I have changed, or will change the way I am looked at and replace it with something else.

And once done I will always see that something else for the way it moves in and out of my gross hands and mouth.

I'm not even sorry for myself, I just am. Un-disgraced ceaseless anger, wanting something, not knowing it by name and having wanted it for a while and that while having been sometimes sliced by pause, sometimes else made horribly present but either way, I know, I put too much hope in not having to tell anybody anything, or maybe constantly having nothing to tell.

There is a point at which the frequency and nature of your communications come close to actually forming a relationship and it is that point I have searched out with scientific care.

I give myself a headache by looking at myself in the mirror real close, but I do it well.

And the bad people will steal from you, even if you become the bad people.

The bad people will steal from you even if you taught them how to be bad people.

There is only one way to imagine things.

And I am part of the thing imagined.

The lesson I learned from the times I thought you were going to say something but didn't, is a lesson I don't remember. Which is part of the thing imagined.

I try hard not to make a difference.

I can only imagine things one way, not having to tell anybody anything, or maybe constantly having nothing to tell.

Yuh huh.

Sam Pink lives in Chicago.

LAZY FASCIST PRESS
2012

The Obese by Nick Antosca

Anatomy Courses by Blake Butler and Sean Kilpatrick

A Parliament of Crows by Alan M. Clark

The Last Final Girl by Stephen Graham Jones

Zombie Bake-Off by Stephen Graham Jones

Chick Bassist by Ross E. Lockhart

The Collected Works of Scott McClanahan Vol. I
by Scott McClanahan

The Devil in Kansas by David Ohle

30 Likely to Die Before 30 edited by Cameron Pierce

I Am Going to Clone Myself Then Kill the Clone and Eat It
by Sam Pink

No One Can Do Anything Worse To You Than You Can
by Sam Pink

A Pretty Mouth by Molly Tanzer

Broken Piano for President by Patrick Wensink

Everything Was Great Until It Sucked by Patrick Wensink

Available at Amazon.com

CPSIA information can be obtained at www.ICGtesting.com
Printed in the USA
BVOW08s0730150116

432997BV00002B/45/P